MORALE MATTERS

A police officer's guide to reducing stress
and improving morale in the workplace

Neville Evans

GW00634937

Bullied Publishing 2011

Morale Matters

A police officer's guide to reducing stress and improving morale in the workplace

Copyright © 2011 Neville Evans

The right of Neville Evans to be identified as the author of the work has been asserted by him in accordance with the copyright, Designs and Patents Act 1988.

The author's views are personal and not the views of South Wales Police.

Published by Bullied Publishing 2011

137 New Road
Porthcawl
Bridgend
CF36 5DD
www.talkandsupport.co.uk
Cover photograph: Thomas Franetti Photography 'Officer at Ease, PC Paul Clute, Metropolitan Police, UK'
Design: Neil Edwards (www.visucreative.co.uk)
With thanks to the Royal College of Psychiatrists, HSE UK and Mind UK.

ISBN 978-0-9561434-2-6

Contents

INTRODUCTION 05

CHAPTER 1: *THE REAL WORLD OF POLICE STRESS* 09
Some definitions 10
Stress 15
The effects of stress, are you stressed? 17
StressMap® 20
The stress response 20
Denial 22
Workaholism 22
Alcohol 24
Exercise 24

CHAPTER 2: *POLICE STRESS AND ITS SOLUTIONS* 27
Hunger and stress 28
Temperature 31
Noise 31
Sleep 32
Seasonal changes and light availability 35
Violence and aggression 36

CHAPTER 3: *THE SOCIAL EFFECTS OF POLICE WORK* 39
Emotional rollercoaster 40

CHAPTER 4: *PSYCHOLOGICAL STRESS AND ITS SOLUTION* 43
Emotional police work 44
Mastering emotional responses the use of mindfulness meditation 51
Time management 57
Thinking about difficult situations 61

CHAPTER 5: *GETTING EXTRA HELP AND SUPPORT* 65
Online life coaching 66
Post-traumatic stress disorder 67
Psychotherapy 73
What is CBT? 76
Trauma risk management 81
Counselling 82

CHAPTER 6: *WORK MORALE AND ITS LINK WITH ORGANISATIONAL STRESS* 85
Demands 88
Support 98
Control 106
Relationships 109
Communication 116
Role 121
Change 122

CHAPTER 7: *ETHICAL POLICING* 127
Reward and punishment 129
The misunderstanding 133
Sex 140
Harming others 140
Theft 141
Dishonesty 141
Malicious speech 142
Covetousness 142
How do police officers introduce the daily practice of ethical motivation? 142
Why do this practice? 149

CHAPTER 8: *REMEMBER THE POSITIVES* 151
Exciting role 152
Freedom to roam 153
Insight knowledge 153
Making a difference 153
Sport and groups 154
Friends 154
Gratitude 154

CHAPTER 9: *CONCLUSION* 155
How do morale, culture, stress and ethics link together? 156

INTRODUCTION

Introduction

The reason for writing this book is to give serving police officers, police staff and senior officers a clear objective view of stress in a real-world policing context. In my writings, I want to expose the difficulties that front-line officers face and approach the principles from the mindset of the officer. This important approach will hopefully serve to give the reader real insight into the officer's thinking and emotional response. When I use the word 'morale', I am referring to positive and negative states of mind.

Here, I will try and offer a more philosophical approach to policing, this will hopefully challenge the vision, aims and objectives culture that policing embraces.

This book takes the perspective of the first person and the third person approach. The first person approach is the actual experience of police officers; this invaluable knowledge will serve to make the 'stress' issue more personable and real. The third person approach is the application of scientific methodology. I will use scientific studies to knit together my theories and writings. Hopefully, by adopting these two approaches, we will see a balanced evidence-based assessment of morale and how it can be improved. The moulding of science, philosophy and real officer experience will serve to provide a positive framework from which to work from.

I detest the word 'responsibility'. It is a word that assumes. I prefer to use 'the ability to respond'; this reversal ensures that we have some choice in our ability to improve our own morale and take control of our 'personal stress'. Some readers may disagree with my writings, what I am proposing is a radical approach that looks at the bigger picture of morale, stress at work, philosophy, ethical decision making, culture and service. I hopefully will be able to link the entire subjects together and explain how all are connected and how they shouldn't be viewed separately but as a collective and dynamic living system.

This book is not an authority on the issue of 'stress and the police officer', if you, the reader, have any recommendations, please feel free to share them. A huge 'thank you' to all the staff at Bridgend Police Station.

Useful Contacts

Samaritans ....

Counsellor ....

Doctors ....

Solicitor ....

Therapist ....

Friends ....

Spiritual ....

Welfare Officer ....

Police Federation ....

Police Supervisor ....

THE REAL WORLD
OF POLICE STRESS

What is stress? What is morale?

Some definitions:

Morale is defined by the Oxford Dictionary as:

> ### 'Morale'
> *The confidence, enthusiasm, and discipline of a person or group at a particular time*

Dr Richard Lazarus, a prominent stress researcher, defines psychological stress as:

> *'A particular relationship between the person and the environment that is appraised by the person as taxing and exceeding his or her resources and endangering his or her well-being'.*

Dr Lazarus emphasises that stress is a transaction between a person and his or her environment. Transaction means to exchange and, in the realms of a stressful event, the deciding coping effect will be determined by the person who is experiencing the stress. A person who has the resources or coping strategies will in effect cope much better than a person who has none.

In the first definition, the qualities of morale are made up of states of being. They assume a shift as the word 'time' is introduced; therefore, morale is an ever-moving concept that moves and changes. It is not a constant. It is an elusive concept. In the second definition, stress is viewed as a changing transaction between the person and environment. The perception of an individual as to what is stressful and what is not rests entirely with the person. Perception is an ever-moving concept that moves and changes. Our thoughts and feelings change from moment to moment. Stress and morale have a relationship with one another. When morale is at its optimum and the confidence and enthusiasm of staff members is high, the aims and objectives of the police service become effortless. When enjoyment and calm infuse individual officers it becomes a joy to face the daily challenges of police work. Confidence and enthusiasm are states of mind; if you take away an individual's confidence and enthusiasm, then the policing environment by its very nature can place officers into a world of inner pressure and stress. Therefore, positive work morale is the first line of defence to the realities of police stress.

Let's begin: The police perspective

To get a real look and feel for morale and stress let's begin with a simple exercise. This exercise works best with a group of colleagues or it can be done on your own. You will need an alarm clock, pen, paper and a chair to sit on. Write on your piece of paper three columns: past, present and future.

Set the alarm clock for five minutes and sit in the chair in a comfortable position. Close your eyes and relax. Just simply breathe in and out for the entire five minutes.

While you are enjoying this time for relaxation, note how your mind wanders. Once the five minutes is up, relax and record what thoughts you had; be honest and record everything. Now record any emotions that registered within you. Splurge all your ideas onto a piece of paper.

Once you finished your personal exercise, join each experience with the rest of the group and record each item on a large board. If you are doing this exercise as an individual, repeat the exercise at different times of the day.

As a group, you will make the following observations:

- ❏ Our thoughts and feelings jump from one topic to another.
- ❏ Our feelings lack depth, they fade and lack momentum.
- ❏ Our inner experiences as a group have no consistency.
- ❏ Our essential nature is a little chaotic and unpredictable.
- ❏ We tried desperately hard to control our minds, but failed.
- ❏ Our minds are restless, they are thinking about the future, the past and rarely about the here and now.

We call this experience and realisation 'the sea of reality'. Our fundamental nature is not as controlled, not as ethical, not as perfect as we would like to think. As the sea is in constant change and flux, so are our minds. By acknowledging that our minds are under constant change, we can begin to understand and accept that our actual day-to-day policing experience is agitated by the choppy and often un-predictable waters of police work. Acknowledgement of our current predicament can be the start of a powerful inner transformation.

The following descriptions give us some insight into our most common thinking patterns:

Forward thinking mind
You may be constantly thinking about the future, planning weeks in advance, thinking about problems before they have surfaced, constantly thinking and planning, going around and around and not getting anywhere.

Worrying mind
Worrying about all manner of projects, family life, work commitments, holidays,

childcare, have you sent that email, have you responded to the last, don't want to lose face, got to keep up appearances. Worrying about decisions made, worrying about what your colleagues will say, will I be criticised? Can I cope with criticism?

Judging mind

My work is better, my approach is more professional. PC Jones turned up late, obviously a dim wit. PC Evans said "So and so", obviously a racist. PC Lloyd is not interested in this case, obviously unprofessional. PC Morris is an attractive girl, I like her, want her on my team. CID are all timewasters. Community policing, not real policing. Domestic violence victims, not real crime. Drug users are absolute scum. Management are out for themselves.

Day-dreaming mind

When I retire, I am going to be happy and get another job, I will enjoy my life and relax every day. I won't be working hard. Only another 20 years to go. I won't have any problems, life will be perfect.

Locked in battle mind

I hate that Inspector. I will do everything I can to discredit him and make him look inferior to me. I will imagine him losing face, I will imagine him slipping up and I will say to him "I told you so". Everyone I meet I will tell them how unpopular he is. I am feeling so angry with him. He is the problem; it's got nothing to do with me.

This exercise is an experiential one and can be used as a tool to record thoughts and feelings during times of high stress and pressure. Employees who conduct this exercise on a weekly basis notice times when stress and pressure peak and trough. This form of personal analysis can serve to identify when and where your main stress is coming from. A personal stress diary is recommended to allow yourself the thinking time to evaluate your own personal weekly stress encounters. By acknowledging that our thinking patterns are a little chaotic, we acknowledge that morale and personal stress change on a moment-by-moment basis. This realisation draws us to the conclusion that 'We must make a daily effort to consider our own and others' morale on a daily basis'. We become aware that although the day looks settled and performance is good, someone in the police service is having a challenging day.

The science behind the wandering mind theory

The mind is a frequent, but not happy, wanderer: people spend nearly half their waking hours thinking about what isn't going on around them. People spend 46.9 percent of their waking hours thinking about something other than what they're doing, and this mind-wandering typically makes them unhappy. So says a study that used an iPhone web app to gather 250,000 data points on subjects' thoughts, feelings, and actions as they went about their lives.

The research, by psychologists Matthew A. Killingsworth and Daniel T. Gilbert of Harvard University, is described in the journal 'Science'.

Unlike other animals, humans spend a lot of time thinking about what isn't going on around them: contemplating events that happened in the past, might happen in the future, or may never happen at all. Indeed, mind-wandering appears to be the human brain's default mode of operation.

To track this behaviour, Killingsworth developed an iPhone web app that contacted 2,250 volunteers at random intervals to ask how happy they were, what they were currently doing and whether they were thinking about their current activity or about something else that was pleasant, neutral or unpleasant.

Subjects could choose from 22 general activities, such as walking, eating, shopping and watching television. On average, respondents reported that their minds were wandering 46.9 percent of the time, and no less than 30 percent of the time during every activity, except making love.

"Mind-wandering appears ubiquitous across all activities," says Killingsworth, a doctoral student in psychology at Harvard. "This study shows that our mental lives are pervaded, to a remarkable degree, by the non-present.

"Mind-wandering is an excellent predictor of people's happiness. In fact, how often our minds leave the present and where they tend to go is a better predictor of our happiness than the activities in which we are engaged."

Time-lag analyses conducted by the researchers suggested that their subjects' mind-wandering was generally the cause, not the consequence, of their unhappiness.

This very recent piece of research when applied to the world of policing raises some very important questions. The police officer, police supervisor and senior police officer constantly has to juggle policing experiences and incidents from one day to the next. This juggling creates the: worrying mind, judging mind, day-dreaming mind and locked in battle mind. This research provides a very valid reason for unhappiness at work. It also asks the question: Are you a happy police officer?

 Does the nature of police work undermine the confidence and enthusiasm of it's officers?

The evidence of police stress

The evidence that police officers are subjected to chronic stress is overwhelming and research has been conducted all over the world. In the UK, 12.8 million days at work were lost due to stress, anxiety and depression between 2004 and 2005.

Collins and Gibbs found that occupational stressors ranking most highly within the population were not specific to policing, but to organizational issues such as the demands of work impinging upon home life, lack of consultation and communication, lack of control over workload, inadequate support and excess workload in general. The high scoring group constituted 41 percent of the population and differed significantly from those with low scores in perception of all stressors, ranking both personal and occupational stressors more highly, and from personality constraints appeared significantly more 'stress-prone'. A significant association between gender and mental ill health was found, with females more likely to score more highly on the General Health Questionnaire than males.

Dr. Barocas B. Gershon estimates the effects of perceived work stress in police officers and determines the impact of coping on both perceived work stress and health. Officers from a large, urban police department (N = 1,072) completed detailed questionnaires. Exposure to critical incidents, workplace discrimination, lack of cooperation among co-workers and job dissatisfaction correlated significantly with perceived work stress. Work stress was significantly associated with adverse outcomes, including depression and intimate partner abuse. **Officers who relied on negative or avoidant coping mechanisms reported both higher levels of perceived work stress and adverse health outcomes.** Results have implications for improving stress-reducing efforts among police officers. Interventions that address modifiable stressors and promote effective coping and resiliency will probably be most beneficial in minimising police stress and associated outcomes.

In Norway, researchers surveyed 3,272 Norwegian police at all hierarchical levels and compared the same results with the same number of Norwegian doctors.

The physical threats in police operational duties have been regarded as inherent causes of stress in police work, but organizational factors such as work overload, time pressure, inadequate resources, manpower shortage, lack of communication, managerial styles etc. emerge as more stressful. This may indicate that police are trained for police operational duties, whereas their ability to cope with organizational stressors may be less adequate.

The negative impact of stress in police work is manifested in different ways, such as somatic and mental health problems and burnout, and it depends on the frequency, the intensity and how the experienced situation is perceived. Data on frequency is important in determining which stressors have had the greatest impact on daily police work.

Previous research has emphasized individual differences when it comes to stress and work. Here, the focus of interest has been in personality factors. Two prominent concepts have been the locus of control and neuroticism. **Neuroticism tends to correlate with psychological distress and is an independent predictor of burnout in police.** Attitudes and behavioural characteristics generated by police work itself can lead to rigidity, suspiciousness, cynicism and authoritarianism, which are attributed to burnout.

The prevalence of subjective health complaints was relatively high and was mainly associated to job pressure and lack of support. Males showed more depressive symptoms than females. Compared with the general population, though, police showed lower mean scores on both anxiety and depressive symptoms. All stress factors on frequency were positively associated to the burnout dimensions depersonalization and emotional exhaustion, except work injuries. The comparisons with physicians showed that they have markedly different emotional reactions to work stress.

Interestingly this research highlights this issue of perception and mechanisms of coping that police do not inherently possess. The constant experience of police work actually increases the behavioural characteristics that lead to chronic stress and burnout. The issue of depression and anxiety with the police service is an issue that individual officers can train and prepare for; modern and exciting research has paved the way for a new health paradigm.

Stress

The word 'stress' implies a condition that we experience at a given moment in time. This viewpoint can be observed in people who suffer from stress. We commonly hear people say "I suffer from stress". "I suffer" is a helpless view point, implying that we are immersed in stress and cannot do anything about. The conditions for a stressful outcome surround us. Stress is based on necessary conditions that become accentuated at certain times that place competing demands up on us. The conditions for stress are known as 'stressors'.

Stressors are numerous and varied, and change from moment to moment. A continuum of stressors exists from extreme stressors such as very bright sunlight (radiation) to the subtle noise of road traffic. Our experience of stressors rests in the awareness of our senses. Awareness is the key ally to perceiving and experiencing stressors. At any given moment we are involved with the interplay of many distracting stressors; however, we are mostly blind to our actual experience. Our daily task-centred life propels us into rushing and 'doing'. We are rarely perceiving, noting and experiencing with the full spectrum of our senses. Our human condition has been extremely well designed to listen with all the senses, but listening has become replaced by doing. We habitually ignore our senses and we plunge our experience of stressors into the deep subconscious of our mind. Stressors build and manifest, and the ignorance of our experience eventually lead us to dis-ease. We are not at ease.

Through our senses, we can identify many potential stressors, these include: hunger and thirst; noise; temperature; smell; taste; touch; feelings; mental characteristics (tiredness, hyperactivity). In addition to physiological stressors, workplace stressors have added to the stress literature.

Government research - HSE Viewpoint

The Health and Safety Executive of the UK has thoroughly researched workplace stress. The research suggests that there are six key areas that managers and staff need to focus on in order to tackle workplace stress. These include:

Change

How organisational change (large or small) is managed and communicated in the organisation.

Role

Whether people understand their role within the organisation and whether the organisation ensures that the person does not have conflicting roles.

Relationships

Includes promoting positive working to avoid conflict and dealing with unacceptable behaviour.

Support

Includes the encouragement, sponsorship and resources provided by the organisation, line management and colleagues.

Demands

Includes issues like workload, work patterns and the work environment.

Control

How much say the person has in the way they do their work.

The research from Norway suggests that these issues are by and large the cause of stress in a policing context; however, prolonged exposure to police work by its very nature is also a predictor of burnout. The Health and Safety Executive's work doesn't take into account our ability to choose activities that can serve to de-stress and heal ourselves. Police work is not comparable to other occupations, it has its own unique set of circumstances. Dr. Gershon, a leader in the field of police officer stress, believes there are two paths to improvement. One is to improve the coping mechanisms of officers who may be exposed to stress, and the other is to identify and address modifiable job stressors. Both of these approaches can help to mitigate the effects of work stress among police officers.

The following paragraphs were written by a serving front-line officer:

"It never ceases to amaze me, take the modern-day police officer's workload. Not only have the police responsibility for crime and disorder, but now anti-social behaviour, environment, communities, mental health, vulnerable persons, street trafficking, terrorism, equality and diversity, hate crime, school bullying, gang culture, missing persons, self harm and suicide.

"When I step out of my world and consider what my colleagues go through each month, it is hard to believe. How many people run to a fight? How many people walk into a burning building? How many people have the tact and empathy when dealing with a victim of rape? Police officers do amazing things every day, prevent someone killing themselves, stop child abuse, return lost children to their loved ones, comfort someone who has lost a relative, catch dangerous and violent criminals, and support victims.

"I laugh with my family sometimes, when they sit and moan about the police. If I wrote about 'a month in the life of a police officer', they would probably say that I made it all up, it is unbelievable what we see and do. In the early days of our service, it's fun racing around to calls, accidents and emergencies. We get a certain buzz, a certain feel of importance and responsibility. After we have reached operational efficiency and have become competent (3–5 years), we may feel that the edge has started to wane. Our willingness to rush and thrive on excitement may lessen. Over time, our experience tells us that before we attend a call we probably can predict an outcome before we have even arrived at the call. Patterns do develop and we become excellent 'doom predictors'. It's a Bank Holiday weekend, full moon and it's been sunny all day. The whole world is enjoying the sun shine, but the police officer waiting to work his night shift is dreading the start of what is going to be a busy one. Better enjoy this cup of tea at the start of the shift, it's going to be your last.

"Over time, and faced with the negativity police work involves, we may feel constantly tired, lethargic and ready to give up. Many colleagues seem to have the world on their shoulders. Burnout is a serious concern for many and can happen to anyone. Sometimes the response of the service can serve to broaden the gap between management and police officers. Motivational talks from senior officers are usually sent via email. They have all the management buzz words 'organisational change', 'transitional period', 'maintaining the high standards that you have set yourself.'"

There seems to be a consistent message 'chin up, we know it's bad, it's your problem, not ours' and then there is the threat of force: 'you may face disciplinary action'. Many beat officers interpret this response as 'no body is listening'. At no time do these motivational talks or communications alter the mindset or improve morale. Trying to impose motivation or sanctions on police officers usually makes the officer even more disgruntled and fed up.

The effects of stress within the police service - The evidence

Scientific studies across the globe have demonstrated that stress is a significant contributor to diseases such as high blood pressure, stroke, diabetes, coronary heart disease, cancer, depression and mental illness.

Stress is significantly correlated with negative emotions such as anger, hostility, anxiety and depression. There is evidence that suppressing emotional expression may play a role in high blood pressure as well as cancer. Depression is a distinctive feature and risk factor with regard to suicide and suicidal thoughts. The evidence relating to police suicide is very mixed and is still being debated.

Dutch researchers showed a significant correlation between the use of force and the perceived use of force in its police officers. When officers felt under pressure they reported feeling justified to use such force.

Stress is strongly correlated with police officer sickness and absenteeism.

American researchers have correlated stress with alcoholism and the divorce rate among police officers.

Researchers at Cardiff University studied the effects of police officer behaviour on the likelihood of domestic violence victims making a formal complaint and supporting a criminal justice response. Victims who were listened to and supported showed higher levels of satisfaction with the police and indeed supported an initial prosecution and follow up with other agencies. Although this research is not linked directly to stress, it paves the way to ask a question. Does police officer morale impact on the general service given to victims of crime? Is there a link between police officer morale and the conviction rate of criminal offenders?

A holistic stress perspective confirms that stress affects every facet of modern-day policing, this includes: ethics, diversity, victim satisfaction, work life balance, absenteeism, performance, police complaints, health and professional conduct.

Recognising stress

Are you stressed?

How you feel

- ❑ Anxious, nervous, worried, frightened
- ❑ Feeling, something dreadful is going to happen
- ❑ Tense, stressed, uptight, on edge, unsettled
- ❑ Unreal, strange, woozy, detached
- ❑ Panicky

How you think

- ❑ Constant worrying
- ❑ an't concentrate
- ❑ Forgetful
- ❑ Lost your sense of humour
- ❑ Thoughts racing
- ❑ Mind jumping from one thing to another
- ❑ Imagining the worst and dwelling on it

Common thoughts

- ❑ "I'm losing control"
- ❑ "I'm cracking up"

- ❑ "I'm going to faint"
- ❑ "My legs are going to collapse"
- ❑ "I'm going to have a heart attack"
- "❑ I'm going to make a fool of myself"
- ❑ "I can't cope"
- ❑ "I've got to get out"

What happens to your body

- ❑ Heart pounds, races, skips a beat
- ❑ Chest feels tight or painful
- ❑ Tingling or numbness in toes or fingers
- ❑ Stomach churning or 'butterflies'
- ❑ Having to go to the toilet
- ❑ Feeling jumpy or restless
- ❑ Tense muscles
- ❑ Body aching
- ❑ Sweating
- ❑ Breathing changes
- ❑ Dizzy, light-headed

What you do

- ❑ Pace up and down
- ❑ Start jobs and not finish
- ❑ Can't sit and relax
- ❑ On the go all of the time
- ❑ Talk quickly or more than usual
- ❑ Snappy and irritable behaviour
- T❑ emper tantrums
- ❑ Drink more
- ❑ Smoke more

- ❏ Eat more (or less)
- ❏ Avoid feared situations

Measuring stress

If you are regularly experiencing some or all of these symptoms, then it is likely that you are experiencing stress. In order to accurately assess stress it is recommended to use the Essi Systems' StressMap®. The StressMap® is the preeminent self-scoring stress assessment tool that assesses your stress level, evaluates your ability to cope with stress, and suggests methods for dealing with stress effectively. Completed in as little as 15 minutes, StressMap Online® helps chart new strategies for enhancing personal health and overall performance.

StressMap Online® includes a comprehensive questionnaire, scoring grid, interpretation guide and action-planning worksheets so you can easily measure your pressures, changes and satisfactions; identify your stress strengths and vulnerabilities; and target areas for improvement in your personal and professional life. NB: There is a cost for this service.

StressMap Online® Features www.essisystems.com/stress_mastery/stressmap/

- ❏ Scientifically based – extensively researched, norm-tested and statistically reliable.

- ❏ Online format – easy to use and can be completed in minutes.

- ❏ Automated – scores and analyses results immediately and automatically.

- ❏ Results-oriented – archives results for easy retrieval and pre- and post-comparisons.

- ❏ Module – can be used as part of an existing health programme or as a standalone assessment tool.

The stress response

Stress is all around us and the job of a frontline police officer places the officer in a set of never-ending stressful circumstances. The external stressors that exist can be controlled or at the very least accepted. The demands on police officers are always changing and sway from chronic stress to acute stress at a moment's notice. It is this reason why the job can be very demanding.

PC John recollects: The police perspective

"It's 8am and a Sunday, the night shift haven't arrested anyone and there are no calls to deal with. Ahh great! Feet up, tea anyone, full breakfast? It doesn't happen very often does it? The next call is different. 'Can a unit attend the black path, a body has been found hanging?' Great, there goes my full English breakfast. So with the inevitable identification, some poor soul has to tell the family that their son is dead.

After tears, consoling and comfort, we leave the call. The next call is different. 'Can a unit attend a call about youths kicking a ball in the street?' After a quick search of the area, the youths aren't found. The elderly complainant meets you at her door. 'I am disabled, I shouldn't have to put up with this, If you don't help me, I am going to have a heart attack.' I was thinking, 'What is this victim talking about? How can such a small issue be so huge? I have just seen a dead man hanging in the trees.'"

The officer's experience two hours ago is now affecting the next call. At a subconscious level this phenomenon can exist after a difficult incident. It may not be a traumatic incident, but there is **significant emotional overlap in day-to-day policing.** This is one of the main reasons why the role of the police officer can be difficult and un-comparable to other occupations.

Imagine it is the start of your set of six shifts. Before the morning shift begins, you're eating breakfast and relaxing, and your partner enters the kitchen. You say good morning and you are greeted with a grunt. Silence and tension remains, all of a sudden an almighty row breaks out. You both are arguing for the sake of arguing. All manner of accusations are made, you both say things that are harsh and full of malice. Doors start to slam, the children begin to cry and you hear "Daddy and Mummy, stop shouting". You storm out of the house and words are said with rage spluttering underneath your breath. You arrive at work in a foul mood. Tension in your heart, fire in your belly. You are fuming with rage.

The pressure, deadlines, emails, telephone calls, customer feedback, meetings and incidents need to be answered. But wait a minute. Ask yourself one question. Can you remain professional and ignore the morning's tirade? Do you need to talk? Do you need to apologise and make sure that you have a home to go back to? We all know that our thinking mind should rationalise this event into a professional outlook and we should be able to separate our work life from our home life. This idea is great in theory, but acknowledging the truth of the situation, we realise that our irrational emotions rule our thinking mind. We can choose to ignore such an honest observation, this is simply suppression. Sometimes the word 'suppression' can get confused with professionalism. Our emotional experiences splurge onto other aspects of our work and home life. This is a natural phenomenon and can be carefully managed with care and patience to oneself.

Chronic stressors involve a long duration and cause slow changes within the body system. The long-term night shift worker is an example of someone who is chronically stressed. Acute stress exhibits itself when a police officer is placed in the height of danger or witnesses something extremely traumatic. Stressors manifest through our senses and work on the physiological, biological and social spectrums. Physiologically, we can become stressed by hunger, thirst, temperature, noise, tiredness, light and atmospheric pressure. Biologically, we are affected by circadian rhythms, seasonal changes and hormones. Socially, we are affected by our workplace, relationships, home life, overtime, policies and procedures. On a daily basis, our entire being is being pulled at from many different angles. The mind-body complex is ingenious, it always wants to return to balance, but our day-to-day living doesn't give us the optimal opportunities for proper rest. Communication is instant, there are more opportunities for activities and we have become busier than our ancestors.

External stressors exhibit their influence on every aspect of our mind-body system, from the cardiovascular system to the immune system.

Once the stressor is signalling via our sense organs, we have a moment of inner contact. The force of the stressor registers an inner stressful event. Imagine attending a call with an armed and violent suspect. Being in the presence of someone threatening exhibits the 'fight or flight' response.

The fight or flight response is a hard-wired response to a threat assessment. Adrenaline is released from the adrenal glands. We become very alert, our heart rate increases and our perception sharpens. The autonomic nervous system releases a chemical cascade of hormones and we prepare to run or fight. This vital capacity becomes problematic when we have no control over its functioning. How many times do police officers get told to stand down from an incident? Does the fight or flight system stand down? On a busy weekend shift this functioning process could be triggered at every call the officer attends. This could be approximately on ten occasions over an eight-hour period. By causing us to react so quickly, the fight or flight reaction often creates problems in the first instance. Stress is contagious; the people we deal with pick up on our hostility and become more hostile. It is this hostility that can cascade and put us in more danger and, consequently, even more stress.

Some police officers are in a state of 'hyperarousal', they are always tense and anxious. They suffer from chronic muscle tension, flushed faces and flaky skin. As a person who works with them, they may be quick to temper and argue at the drop of a hat.

Police officers can take advantage of the fight or flight mechanism in certain circumstances, there are times where we have to fight and maintain social order. For the majority of circumstances, we have to keep our cool and show utter professionalism. We still feel threatened, hurt, resentful, angry and pissed off. We still have those stress hormones floating about. We cope by suppressing those feelings, by denying their very existence. The tough, shielded exterior protects us from emotion. There is mounting evidence that chronic overstimulation of the sympathetic nervous system leads to high blood pressure, sleep disorders, anxiety and creates even more stress.

Many people cope with stress in ways that are actually self destructive. 'Maladaptive coping' is the term used to describe self-destructive behaviour.

Denial

Uncomfortable experiences, thoughts and emotions include a large element of denial. Denial involves awareness or a process of unconscious habit. You may be aware and consciously know that you are hurting but you make the choice to bury the pain that you are experiencing. The decision to do this is usually made as it's the only way you knew of coping. Unconscious habit is an automatic response to uncomfortable feelings that bypasses awareness and places the feeling deep into the body.

In a recent study, Dr. Gershon and his colleagues found that perceived work stress was strongly associated with avoidant and negative coping behaviours. 'One interesting finding from this study was that officers reporting high work stress and who relied on avoidant coping mechanisms were more than 14 times more likely to report anxiety and more than nine times more likely to report burnout than were officers who did not rely on avoidance as a coping strategy.'

In the course of your duties, you would have met countless individuals who just react and hit out in the response to feeling threatened. These individuals have no control when they commit a crime; they are engaged in unconscious habit. The mind has a knack of reminding us that a stressful experience has an emotional and painful component embedded within it. It is this feeling that we avoid most certainly; however, we usually project this feeling onto someone else and we make them the problem.

Emotions cannot be scientifically measured. However, scientists can measure the effect of emotions by measuring their effect on the body. For example, fear can increase your heart rate, adrenaline or blood pressure. The only scientific tool that has been developed to measure real emotions is called the 'human being'. You can do it easily. All you need to do is find a quiet place, sit and relax. Find a breathing space for 15 minutes. If you have decided that you are angry, breathe deeply and concentrate on the inner feeling. Revisit the experiences that made you feel angry and hold the feeling of anger in your mind. In your mind, compare the feeling of anger with the 'tick-tock' of an old-fashioned alarm clock. Give the emotion of anger a numerical value. Breathe deeply, inhaling for four seconds and exhaling for four seconds. Visualise with time; the alarm clock slowing and the inner vibration easing.

When we learn to play a musical instrument, we attribute a particular sound or vibration with a particular note. A skilled musician will be able to listen to the sound and tell you what the note is. In the same way, feelings (inner vibrations) become the sounds and you become the musician. You can now give each emotion a name and recognise how it feels and what qualities it possesses.

This very simple exercise allows you to tune in with how you are feeling. Having witnessed people in distress in your police career, have you noticed that they exhibit the same behaviour? When people are in distress, they find it difficult to communicate their feelings. Emotions are generally described using words, and this is where we fall down. Emotions are not words.

Denial doesn't allow the mind to evaluate what is really happening in the here and now. Whilst we engage with denial, we may find other practices that consume our thoughts. We may become excessively busy and find another task to concentrate on or we may find another coping strategy. Coping strategies are usually taught or modelled. Denial is a large part of society. Statements like 'Big boys don't cry' don't help. Hyper-masculine role models show little understanding of the relationship of mind and body. They are usually too busy avoiding what is actually hurting them.

Workaholism is a classic coping strategy. Many people throw themselves into work and create their own working identities. Work becomes an excuse not to develop the other aspects of your life and in the eyes of many you become the committed professional, the leader, the one who inspires and has never had a day sick. Bosses sometimes place this burden upon themselves and work late hours in the fear of being called 'weak or uncommitted'. Within certain departments it becomes the norm to work late for the love of the job. A culture can form and everybody becomes stressed!

Alcohol

After working a busy shift, the workaholic comes home to rest. The family are asleep; the peace and quiet is unbearable. The mind is racing and the sights and sounds whizz literally around the officer's head. The officer cannot believe what was experienced today. Why can't the world be peaceful for one moment? The officer reaches out for the first sip of cold beer, instant calmness and a warm glow surrounds him in the security of his own home. It is only time and volume before the inner world becomes relaxed and soft again. Such is the grip and ease of alcohol. Research has shown that alcoholism is a large part of global police culture. Alcohol is legal, cheap and easy to get hold of. Many health campaigns depict alcohol as the culprit for disease, but this blameful approach is incorrect. It is our stressed minds and coping mechanisms that create the need for alcohol, and once 'need' has been created we then move to actioning our behaviour.

Exercise

Police officers are always going to extremes; running marathons, swimming across the channel and raising monies for charities. Exercise can be an excusable lure for stressed individuals. Nobody comments on fitness fanatics. More is better and healthier, and it is this reason why exercise dangers can go unnoticed. Exercise, when used disproportionately, can cause all sorts of physiological problems. Officers complain of bad backs, joint problems and are constantly physically tired. Intense physical exercise is not beneficial for individuals in the long run. The key to stress-reducing exercise is the prescription of a lifestyle choice. Healthy exercise involves spontaneity, fun and, above all, a feeling of being lost in the moment. Choose an exercise choice that involves others, improves your sociability and fosters a relaxing element. Avoid unnecessary physical punishment and activities that seem to be goal orientated. Goal-orientated exercise adds pressure to the exercise experience. Instead of enjoying the experience, we can become caught up in judging and evaluating our performance. Examples include: basketball, five-a-side football, surfing, yoga, gardening, badminton, Pilates, circuit training, indoor climbing etc.

Maladaptive coping strategies such as alcohol, drugs, exercise, smoking, food and workaholism provide temporary relief from short-term problems. However, long-term dependency contributes to a compounded stress response. A person who eventually breaks down may have to contend with emotional problems, but also alcohol dependency and a range of other issues. Our emotional reactions and moods have been habituated, trained and conditioned to respond in certain ways. The first step in undermining this conditioning is to realise for ourselves the role of the stress response and the unconscious decisions that we make and which maladaptive solutions we immerse ourselves in.

Continued exposure to police work, harmful emotional responses and the rollercoaster ride of maladaptive coping eventually leads to burnout, sickness and ill health. Breakdown in the stress response does not have to be physical, it could lead to a nervous breakdown. A point in our lives where total psychological exhaustion causes us to withdraw from life altogether. The healthy alternative to the stress-reaction cycle is to stop reacting to stress and start responding to it.

Western psychology is somewhat young in comparison to Eastern psychology and philosophy. At this present time, there seems to be dialogue and research that overlaps both types of thinking. Much research and debate has paved the way towards a more holistic sense of psychology or mind science. In the past ten years, behavioural medicine has dominated the headlines and some of the research has massive implications for workplaces of the future. Behavioural medicine recognizes that our thought patterns and emotions play a significant role in health and disease.

Historically, personality was confined to immovable character traits that predicted whether you would behave in a particular way. This focus was made more viable with the study of genetics and the gene code, many doctrines have passed and there isn't a global consensus on how our mind works. However, with the advent of neuroscience, personality is now regarded as a malleable concept. This means through training in positive thinking processes, our general disposition and outlook can change. This is welcomed news that we can improve our mental health and general well-being. In the very first exercise, you became aware of how uncontrollable the mind can be, but with training this process can eventually change.

Dr. Martin Seligman, an American researcher, has been studying the health differences between people who are either pessimistic or optimistic. His overall findings conclude that optimism has a protective effect against depression, illness and premature death.

We are now no longer helpless and we do have a certain level of say in how our lives unfold. This dawn of positive psychology comes with the general understanding that it is now up to you to make progress and make the determined effort to live a less-stressful life. But as great as ideas are, is this achievable in the modern-day police service? After all, in the last 30 years, technology has brought its new problems, society can contact us at a moment's notice and we have more legislation to deal with offenders. Lower police numbers, increased workload and the general problems that a police officer endures ensure increased stress, sickness and ill health. Over the past 30 years, there has been significant improvement in the way in which police services tackle officer safety and conflict management. Police injury and mortality rates across the globe have decreased as a result of technological and tactical developments. However, in comparison, sickness and mental health issues have increased and therefore we can conclude that emotional survival is an aspect of policing that has been taken for granted. The tide has to turn and the police staff member must be given the compassion, space and training tools that ensure a managed response to stress and mental health problems.

CHAPTER SUMMARY

Police stress comprises:

❏ individual emotional responses – police officers who relied on negative or avoidant coping mechanisms reported both higher levels of perceived work stress and adverse health outcomes;

❏ organisational culture – including exposure to critical incidents, workplace discrimination, lack of cooperation among co-workers, and job dissatisfaction correlated significantly with perceived work stress;

❏ workplace issues – such as the demands of work impinging upon home life, lack of consultation and communication, lack of control over workload, inadequate support and excess workload in general.

The next chapters focus on physiological, psychological and workplace stressors, and give current scientific solutions to each stressor, culminating in the practice of mindfulness meditation for stress reduction.

Unhappiness + low morale + stress = poor performance + ill health + absenteeism + unethical conduct

POLICE STRESS
AND ITS
SOLUTIONS

Physiological stressors

Physiological stressors include hydration, food, temperature, noise, sleep, light, violence, seasonal changes, daily changes and fitness. It may seem obvious to some that I have included the very basic stressors, but it doesn't surprise staff that on a daily basis it is these issues which are not considered by frontline police officers and supervisors. The stress reaction doesn't work in unison when we consider police work. When a major incident happens, officers work overtime, through the night and ignore issues such as hydration and energy levels. It is the compounding of stressors that leads to a stress response. It is no wonder that the day later mistakes are noticed and commented on.

Hunger and stress

In the UK police service, meal breaks and refreshments are subject to the exigencies of duty (police regulations). The word 'exigencies' means an urgent need or demand. This means that if an officer is called upon to impart urgent duties then a meal break doesn't need to be provided at that moment in time, but once the need has been met, a refreshment break has to be provided. This regulation can be interpreted as not needing to consider staff meal breaks or refreshments, and of course this is incorrect. Frontline staff continually complain about this issue, it does become difficult to ensure when staffing numbers are low and the calls keep flooding in. Research shows that hunger causes an adverse stress response. Hungry people usually subconsciously choose foods that are higher in calorific value and therefore this response compounds the weight problem. Officers eat more calories and the food choices becomes less healthy, the stress response then begins to cycle. Hunger stress affects obesity levels. The solution to hunger stress rests in the work time preparations. Bringing small snacks to work increases the opportunity for eating on the go. Experienced officers will usually have a dry cupboard in their lockers full of easily cooked foods (cous cous, rices, dried fruits, tinned food etc). Traditionally, the start of the policing shift is the time where demand is less and therefore a time where food can be consumed in relative peace. It is advised to eat before the shift begins; leaving meal times later entertains an element of risk. Cooking for your family members can be easily accommodated by the use of a slow-cooker. These ingenious devices can cook a variety of meals for the busy police household and there always seems to be enough food left over for freezing or storing for the very next day. A skilful supervisor knows that an 'army marches on its stomach' and will ensure that every shift member is allocated the appropriate time to refuel.

It's generally accepted that how we feel can influence what we choose to eat or drink (mood to food). What is less well known is how what we eat can affect our mental functioning (food to mood). The use of caffeine is one example of a complex relationship. Caffeine, found in tea, coffee, cola drinks and chocolate, is probably the most widely used behaviour-modifying drug in the world. We often choose to drink it if we are feeling tired and irritable, because it can give us a boost and help us to concentrate. Having a cup of coffee or tea also has a lot of positive psychological associations. We meet a friend for 'coffee and a chat' or give ourselves a break by sitting down with a cup of tea, and these things are very important. But too much caffeine (which is a different amount for each of us) can cause symptoms, such as anxiety, nervousness and depression. Any exploration into food and mood needs to take into account this two-way relationship and include the psychological aspect behind what we are choosing to eat.

How do I find out if food is affecting my emotional health?

Before investigating the specific foods that could be affecting your emotional health, it's well worth having a look at what you are already eating and drinking. Usually, the most reliable way of doing this is to keep a food and drink diary every day, for about one week. It seems to work best if you can write down what you eat and drink, at the time you have it. The more information you include in your diary, the more useful it is likely to be; for example, you could also note down the time and the approximate amounts you consume. People are often surprised when they look back over what they have eaten. Greater awareness is an important first step forward.

What should I look for in my diet?

A fundamental thing for you to consider will be: is there any one food or type of food that I eat nearly every day or in particularly large amounts? The basis of a healthy diet is about achieving a balance between a wide variety of foods, where the variety is spread out over a number of days. Certain foods are eaten on most days, by most people, perhaps because they are generally considered healthy to eat. Unfortunately, these can be the very foods that are having a disguised, yet disabling, influence upon your health.

It's often a combination of eating too much of some foods and not enough of others that is contributing to symptoms such as depression or anxiety. An essential part of making changes to your diet involves making sure you are not going without the nutrients your body requires on a daily basis. So, if you cut down on one food, you will usually need to substitute something similar to eat, instead. This may mean, for example, replacing wheat-based bread with bread made from rye flour.

Which foods affect which moods?

The precise cause-and-effect relationship between different foods and moods has yet to be scientifically established, but many people have found they can link eating (or not eating) certain foods with how they feel. The foods and drinks that most often cause problems are those containing alcohol, sugar, caffeine, chocolate, wheat (such as bread, biscuits, and cakes), dairy products (such as cheese), certain artificial additives (or E numbers) and hydrogenated fats. Other commonly eaten foods, such as yeast, corn, eggs, oranges, soya and tomatoes, may also cause symptoms for some people, sometimes.

Significant improvement to a wide range of mental health problems can result from making changes to what we eat. There have been reports of improvements in the following: mood swings, anxiety, panic attacks, cravings or food 'addictions', depression (including postnatal depression), irritable or aggressive feelings, concentration, memory difficulties, premenstrual syndrome (PMS), insomnia, fatigue and Seasonal Affective Disorder (SAD).

Which foods do I need to eat in order to feel well?

The most vital substance for a healthy mind and body is water. It's easy to overlook drinking the recommended six to eight glasses, per day, which is a low-cost, convenient, self-help measure that can quickly change how we feel, mentally as well as physically. Having a minimum of five portions, daily, of fresh fruit and vegetables (organically grown, if possible) provides the nutrients needed to nourish mind and body (one portion equals about a handful).

It's best not to skip breakfast, to keep regular meal times, and to choose foods that release energy slowly, such as oats and unrefined wholegrains. It's also important to eat some protein foods, such as meat, fish, beans, eggs, cheese, nuts or seeds, every day. As well as providing nutrients, these eating strategies help smooth the negative effects of fluctuating blood sugar levels, which include irritability, poor concentration, fatigue, depression and food cravings. Essential fatty acids, particularly the omega-3 type found in oil-rich fish, such as mackerel and sardines, linseeds (flax), hemp seeds and their oils, are vital for the formation and healthy functioning of the brain. Other seeds and nuts, such as sunflower seeds, pumpkin seeds, Brazil nuts and walnuts, also contain important 'good mood' nutrients.

How can I go about changing my diet?

It's probably a lot easier if you start by making changes slowly, one at a time, and just for a trial period. Changing what you eat takes a bit of effort and time; trying out new and different foods may mean you need to shop in new places. Hopefully, you will enjoy making these changes and find them to be a positive experience. Smaller changes, introduced one at a time, are easier to manage and keep up, should you find them beneficial. If you make more than one change at a time, then you won't be able to tell what is having an effect! Some changes may even be unnecessary, although you won't know until you try. This step-by-step approach can be broadened out later, and keeping a food and mood diary may be helpful.

Sometimes, a change to the diet produces some unpleasant side effects, for the first few days only. If people suddenly stop drinking coffee, for instance, they may get withdrawal symptoms, such as headaches, which then begin to clear up after a few days, when they start to feel much better. Symptoms such as these can be reduced if you cut down gradually, rather as if you were weaning yourself from a drug. There are, necessarily, some costs associated with making changes to what you eat, but these can be rewarded by significant benefits to mental and physical health.

Temperature

During working hours, the temperature in all workplaces inside buildings shall be reasonable. This advice is ambiguous as the perception of temperature depends on a variety of personal factors such as perception, personal protective equipment, uniform policies, humidity and hydration. Police work is highly changeable and there are examples of police officers environments changing in both extremes. If you are feeling hot and bothered by wearing a tie in the summer with the burden of PPE, ask your fellow shift members and write a group report. Explain that you are feeling uncomfortable in the hot weather and ask to request a risk assessment and staff questionnaire. This will compel management to seriously consider such requests. During seasonal change it is a good idea to have at your disposal adequate uniform in your work locker. Keep a spare set of clothes, gloves, long johns, batteries, hand warmers, waterproofs and torches. Consider an air-tight bag for clothing contaminated by CS spray. During the summer period consider wearing lightweight boots or shoes and carry a water bottle.

The type of uniform that police officers wear isn't conducive to environmental needs of the police officer. Looking professional can be seen to outweigh the need for personal comfort. Police officers have had a military type of training exposure and this exposure has brought about certain norms. Crew cut hair styles, polished boots, tie and shirts pressed. Looking professional certainly doesn't mean acting professional. This approach is old-fashioned and ritualistic.

Research has shown that caring, compassionate police officers can leave a lasting effect on domestic violence victims, it is the good listener that can literally talk a victim into providing a statement of complaint. Uniformed presence doesn't alter the victim's mindset, but intimate listening does.

The UK police helmet was designed over 100 years ago and it hasn't altered much. The basic police helmet could be designed with an inbuilt camera and could have many smart applications. Uniform hasn't evolved with materials science and remains basic and traditional. Police uniforms are about traditional image and not about police officer comfort. We are taught that communication is mostly non-verbal and emanates in calm, persuasive body language. Body language is the police officers biggest ally in the fight against crime. However, hot, stressed and uncomfortable police officers rarely show the composure that makes operational policing easier. The control of comfort and temperature will allow police officers the necessary start to a calm outlook, which will hopefully resonate into calm and composed body language.

Noise

Noise can have a detrimental effect on our health in the long term, but in the short term, it isn't something that police officers plan for or consider. When policing a busy city centre in the midst of a drunken football match, it is surprising how much noise the environment and public houses emit. People shout VERY LOUDLY when they are drunk. The night club scene emits low frequency noise in the form of 'BOOM,

BOOM'. It is also a time when emergency services are busier and the radio keeps on spluttering out information. Custody staff are subject to continual noise by the nature of loud and demanding detainees, continually shouting and banging on cell doors.

Research has shown that chronic noise exposure is associated with a mildly to moderately increased risk of heart attack. The increase appears more closely associated with actual sound levels rather than with subjective annoyance. Researchers theorise that noise affects the stress response cycle and may be spiking the fight or flight response.

The solution to continual noise is the daily use of an ear piece. The QUIETPRO earplug developed by Nacre, a Norwegian company, may be the answer. This clever ear piece counteracts background noise and only allows talking commands to be amplified. In many high-pressured policing scenarios, communication is somewhat hampered by background noise. Examples include public order situations, fire arms operations, motorway policing, demonstrations etc. This device will not only reduce the risk of noise, but also improve 'stressful' communication.

Sleep

Sleep amongst police officers is a daily complaint and it is this issue that affects so many police officers' lives. Recent studies are showing a worrying health trend for police officers and police staff. Given this new research, is there anything that police officers can do to restore some balance?

People with chronic stress report shorter sleep duration, worsening sleep quality, and more daytime functioning impairments, according to new research. Conversely, daytime functioning impairments and shorter sleep duration demonstrated a predictive relationship with habitual stress complaints.

Nurses participating in shift work, especially those working rotating shifts, face a significantly increased risk of developing Irritable Bowel Syndrome (IBS) and abdominal pain compared to those working a standard daytime schedule, according to research published in the American Journal of Gastroenterology.

A sampling of police officers shows a high incidence of sleep disorders among the members of this profession. Sleep disorders are common, costly and treatable, but often remain undiagnosed and untreated. Unrecognised sleep disorders adversely affect personal health and may lead to chronic sleep loss, which, in turn, increases the risk of accidents and injuries. These problems are exacerbated in shift workers such as police officers, who may experience chronic sleep loss due to their schedules. A sampling of police officers shows a high incidence of sleep disorders among the members of this profession, according to recent research.

A new study published in the current issue of Archives of Environmental & Occupational Health (vol. 64, No. 3) shows that this combination of night work, overtime and shortened sleep can contribute to the development among police officers of the metabolic syndrome, a combination of unhealthy factors that increase the risk of cardiovascular disease (CVD), primarily heart disease and stroke.

Speaking to police officers who have worked shifts for a period of ten years or more, it seems that there are some widely different practices. PC John shares her advice:

"I prepare my body clock before the night shift by staying up late for the afternoon shifts, I can't go to sleep after my shift so I stay up and watch television with a couple of beers."

PC Cronin says: "I go for a walk with the dog after nights and calm down mentally, I can then usually go to sleep".

PC Evans says: "On a night shift, I usually go for a walk in the early hours, I find it relaxing listening to nature. When the sun is bright, I usually go and watch the sun rise."

Everyone needs sleep. It is almost as important to your health and well-being as food. Although your body always makes sure it gets enough sleep to survive, getting enough sleep to feel refreshed, alert and ready to face the day isn't so easy. Most people need between six to eight hours of sleep. The amount of sleep can be affected by comfort, light, sound, hunger, stress, illness, alcohol and exercise.

The daytime and night-time routine is an important build up to getting those all-important hours. Getting into a routine that sets your body clock is an important step. Experiment with your sleep and record your moods and feelings after waking up from an afternoon shift and night shift. It is important to make adjustments to your way of life. Working shifts is not normal and your needs are greater than the average population. Families and partners need to understand that your rest differs from theirs. Talk to them or even ask them to read this book.

Day shift preparations

Sleep preparations for a normal day would look, realistically, like this:

Early dinner 6pm

Eating at regular times will ensure that your hunger and thirst responses are in line with your sleeping patterns. The type of food is also something to consider. A hot curry at a late time is only going to make you feel uncomfortable and restless.

Activity 7pm

Whatever activity that you are involved in, make sure it isn't hugely stressful or frantic, light exercise or hobbies are recommended. Moderate activity is best.

Relaxation 8pm

You work hard and every day you deserve some form of relaxation. It could be a simple body massage, listening to soothing music or even try some simple breathing meditation. Avoid drinking alcohol or taking any form of stimulant, e.g., caffeine.

Try savouring the scent of lemon, mango, lavender, or other fragrant plants. Scientists in Japan are reporting the first scientific evidence that inhaling certain fragrances alter gene activity and blood chemistry in ways that can reduce stress levels. Instead of a sleeping pill or a mood enhancer, a nose full of jasmine from Gardenia jasminoides could also help.

In collaboration with Dr. Olga Sergeeva and Prof. Helmut Hass from the Heinrich Heine University in Düsseldorf, researchers from Bochum led by Prof. Hanns Hatt have discovered that the two fragrances Vertacetal-coeur (VC) and the chemical variation (PI24513) have the same molecular mechanism of action and are as strong as the commonly prescribed barbiturates or propofol. They soothe, relieve anxiety and promote sleep.

Calm the mind before sleep time, avoid watching television, studying or reading.

Warm bath 9pm

A warm bath has been scientifically proven to help with inducing a sleepy psycho-physiological response.

Bedtime preparations 10pm

You will need a thermometer, fan, blackout blinds, water, earplugs, night mask and suitable bedding. Your room should be as dark as possible, cool and comfortable. Earplugs are an easy way of cutting out background noise. Prior to bedtime, adopt a routine that is pleasant on the mind. Dwell on the day's achievements, think about all the positives in your life and gently drift off into a deep sleep. Focus on the rise and fall of your breath.

Arise at the same time every day or after every shift

You will know how much sleep you require after working till the early hours of the morning or working a night shift. Notice how your moods change after working late shifts. Set your soothing alarm clock to this set time, give yourself time to rest. Try not to make large commitments for the following day and always take into account your current tiredness level. A sleep and mood diary would help you identify the times when you require more rest and recuperation.

Consider your hunger and hydration levels

After working a late shift or night shift, you may need to hydrate yourself prior to going to sleep. When you wake up, this consideration is always worth remembering. In effect, you would have missed breakfast and may not have eaten during your night shift.

Adjust your sleeping times after working your night shifts

The day after a night shift consider allowing yourself more sleep time in order to compensate for your sleep loss.

Consider a daytime nap

Researchers have shown that a 10–20-minute daytime power snooze can have important health and work-related benefits. Studies have shown that napping improves memory and thinking function. Sleep acts as a clear-out phase for our short-term memory.

Night shift preparations

Follow exactly the same relaxation routine for any normal day; however, aim to sleep a minimum of one hour prior to starting the night shift. This period allows for the previous shift's lack of sleep to be compensated for and for a period of rest prior to the night shift. Try not to eat a heavy meal prior to the night shift as this will induce sleepiness. During the shift, a steady level of blood sugar needs to be maintained. Eating small snacks is advised, for example, fruit, toast and cereals. Caffeine at optimal dosage will improve your levels of concentration; however, too much caffeine will disrupt your sleep when you return home. Allow a period of rest at 4am, this is when the body's function is at its lowest. Greet the end of the shift with the sun rising, this will induce the mind's wakeful response.

Afternoon shift preparations

Follow exactly the same relaxation routine for any normal day; however, aim to have an afternoon nap. Prior to starting the shift you should be well fed and relaxed.

Counteracting wakefulness

Waking in the middle of the night is a common experience for shift workers. If you do wake, acknowledge your thoughts and feelings at that moment. Focus on the feeling of your breath and gently notice the rising and falling of your chest. A number of questions may arise. Why am I awake? What time is it? How much time before I go to work? There may be tension in your chest area. Your worries may be surfacing. Try the following strategies:

If you are worrying: Write down your worries on a piece of paper and reinforce your decision to keep your worries on a piece of paper at this time.

If you are concerned about how much sleep you have had: Place your alarm clock in a hard-to-reach place, try to avoid looking at the time. Time is not important, it is not a race to feel refreshed and alert, be gentle with yourself.

If you have had a difficult dream: Allow the dream's feeling to pass and watch your thoughts and feelings gradually eddy out. Watch with curiosity this natural phenomenon.

Seasonal changes and light availability

If you notice that your mood, energy level and motivation take a nosedive each November only to return to normal in April, you may have Seasonal Affective Disorder (SAD). Proper diagnosis is needed by a qualified health care professional.

The most common type of this mood disorder occurs during the winter months. SAD is thought to be related to a chemical imbalance in the brain, brought on by lack of light due to winter's shorter days and typically overcast skies. This condition, characterized by depression, exhaustion and lack of interest in people and regular activities, interferes with a person's outlook on life and ability to function properly, but people should not despair, because SAD is treatable. Police officers with light disruptive sleeping patterns during the night shift period will typically lose two or more days of natural light during the winter months.

With less exposure to light in the winter months, many people become depressed. People susceptible to SAD are affected even more so. If at all possible, get outside during winter, even if it is overcast. Expose your eyes to natural light for one hour each day. At home, open the drapes and blinds to let in natural light. SAD can be effectively treated with light therapy, antidepressant medication and/or psychotherapy. The latest treatment is a headband containing mounted lights that delivers light to your retina whether you are inside or outdoors.

Violence and aggression

It is the job; it's what we deal with. The threat of violence lies with operational police officers every working day. Even though it is tough, this single issue cannot be ignored, it has to be accepted and monitored. Violence by its very nature induces the stress response and thus the flight or fight response. Acknowledging and being receptive to the inner bombardment of thoughts, emotions and hormonal changes allows us to have choice in our response. When we have choice, we are in control.

Police officer training has improved dramatically over the last number of decades. The advent of new training methods, body armour, taser and easy and simple tactics aids to reduce the daily threat of violence. There are many factors that are interrelated to threat and stress. The holistic concept of stress reduction should in theory reduce the intensity and probability of violence. The first few years of being a police officer are probably the most enjoyable. The fast pace, adrenaline-based call to action has many important side effects. When we are threatened, we become aroused, our senses sharpen and our sympathetic nervous system illicit a natural feeling of euphoria or a 'high'. Racing to calls and being the one in the heat of the moment can literally become addictive. Not all police officers are put off by violence and aggression, some actually enjoy the challenge and 'high' that conflict brings. After a tactical team is deployed to search a house or smash down a door, how many times do you observe these officers laughing and joking? After the initial stress and confrontation, officers will reconvene in the backyard of the police station and actively recreate the entire scenario. It is simply the art of telling 'war stories' and police officers love to tell war stories.

The process of talking and re-living the moment is an important aspect of conflict management training. Experiential learning is taking place and officers are engaging in constructive and safe feedback. Things may have gone wrong and it is important to share those learning experiences. Usually humour and banter dominate the group. This again is really positive and shows strong team work and the foundations for trustful relationships develop.

What happens when the officer finishes his tour of duty? The highs and stories of the day seem quite distant from a quiet home. Police officers experience a plunge in emotional well-being and it takes time to unwind and relax after a hectic shift. A bottle of beer becomes more appealing. One drink becomes two and so on, but with the unwinding of the day comes the seesaw of the emotional rollercoaster. The officer is unaware that following a highly stressed incident, the stress response dips. Every action has an equal or opposite reaction and, simply, what goes up must come down. Unwittingly, the officer has added alcohol to the coming down of the emotional rollercoaster. This may be coupled with sleep deprivation and a lack of food. The stress response is magnified. But it doesn't stop there; socialization is another concept that adds to the stressed police culture. The dip of the rollercoaster creates a void, and it is this void that needs to be filled once again.

Socialization

Joining the police service, I was amazed by how it was the norm to go and drink as much alcohol as possible. Everybody would go out and get drunk after the notorious afternoon shift. Everyone would talk about work, stories would be swapped, moans aired and differences settled. The addictive nature of police work was so obvious. A good police officer was one who worked all the hours, never went home, arrested loads of people and was 100 miles per hour on the frontline. Where are they now? In only ten years they have disappeared to an office environment. Why? It's addictive being someone in the face of the public and getting a buzz from the demands of police work. Younger officers love the job and are always at the police station, it's difficult to tell them to go home. I am concerned about the effects of this buzz and its effects on family life; it literally translates into workaholism and can lead to emotional burnout. Police officers need to consider an effective work-life balance and be aware of the pitfalls of living on the 'high' of police work.

An effective work-life balance considers giving time to old friends, exercise, family, creative pursuits, childcare, nature and relaxing pastimes.

The need to belong and be accepted in a group translates into pressure and this has a powerful influence on younger officers. The need to prove yourself and show your commitment has disastrous consequences. How many times have I listened to people boasting about how many arrests they have made or the amount of hours they have worked? It's commonplace and it is an accepted part of police culture. It sometimes sounds like the 'my dad is bigger than your dad' argument that school children engage in. Police officers are naturally competitive and want to prove themselves; they never want to be seen as weak or passive. Performance measurement has added to the stress phenomenon. Arrest, stop and search, and intelligence submissions have added a further dimension to proving an individual's worth. Police officers focus on the end result. "I had 20 arrests last week and I am a great police officer!" The huge issue with this short-term approach is grounded in two considerations.

If the norms of the shift are the middle of the road arrest rates, then the shift will never try and better these statistics, the group will collude together. If the norms of the shift are high, this may make officers engage in unethical practice, stress will overload and the shift will start to 'in fight'. However, if you scrap performance indicators and focus on quality investigations, interviews, statements, forensic opportunities and customer service, you are effectively paving the way for quality to prevail. Quality isn't stressed, it is ethically observant and smart. Performance indicators go against the whole philosophical notion that police officers are paid to 'observe'.

Performance indicators create a ceiling; they stop real creativity and problem solving to spontaneously arise. Incidentally, it's creativity and problem solving that can really improve performance.

The cycle of the police 'high', work socialization and performance indicators align the police culture to a chronically stressed culture. The antidotes include training officers to relax and de-stress, improving work-life balance and paying lip service to performance indicators. Quality is the new performance indicator.

CHAPTER SUMMARY

Physiological stressors, such as hunger, thirst, sleep, rest, temperature and light, change your thinking and behaviour. However, you do have many opportunities to counteract their effect.

3

THE SOCIAL
EFFECTS OF
POLICE WORK

In the book 'Emotional survival for law enforcement', Dr Kevin M. Gilmartin puts forward a very real and valid theory of why police officers become disgruntled, angry and cynical. Dr Kevin M. Gilmartin's theory stems from the inner effects of hypervigilance whilst on duty and the opposing effects of detachment in the off duty stage. Whilst police officers are on duty, they have to develop a distrust of what people are saying and doing. This distrust allows police officers to develop the necessary independent observation skills that keep daily investigation detached and fair. Hypervigilance and distrust also provide the necessary 'thinking processes' that keep police officers alive. If police officers switch off awareness they put themselves and their colleagues at risk. Hypervigilance is a state of mind that is chronically tense and aware. It takes considerable concentration and effort to maintain this state of mind. Whilst rushing to emergency calls, dealing with violent perpetrators and facing aggression and hostility, police officers allow hypervigilance and its effects to help with fast and responsive decisions. Whilst the hypervigilance stage has passed, police officers experience a 'high'. Alertness, quick thinking and adrenaline are providing an elevation in mood. Without thinking about this effect, police officers can literally become addicted to the high of emergency work. The hypervigilance stage takes 18–24 hours to subside. During the off duty stage, police officers experience a corresponding dip in mood. They report feelings of isolation, low mood, tiredness and lethargy. The off duty stage in young officers' careers becomes boring, discontented and mundane. Where would you rather be? A place where your senses are elevated and alert or at home where you feel lethargic and bored? Dr Kevin M. Gilmartin calls this predictable duality the 'Biological Rollercoaster'.

The off duty stage is at the lower spectrum of the roller coaster, it can effect police officers in many ways. When you come home and relax are there certain effects that you have noticed? Does it take time for you to unwind and relax? Do you have meaningless conversations and agree with the person who is talking just for a quiet life? Do you find yourself making excuses for spending time at home? Does your home life seem boring when compared to your police life? Do you avoid people? Do you make contact or pop into the police station, just to find out what has happened? Are you looking forward to going back to work?

The upper spectrum of the rollercoaster opens new opportunities. You start to socialise with your new team, you begin to become accepted within the social ranks of the service. It is noticed how you never say no, always stay to the end and are eager every day. Almost without knowing, you are accepted into the band of brothers. You are respected, a real police officer who can be relied upon. Your conversation changes, it's all police talk, police work, police relationships, police scandal, police, police, police. As this world engulfs you, your old life passes you by. Your views change, your language changes, even your dress code. You lose your old friends and your old identity. Your old identity had many facets; you were a surfer, photographer, artist, comedian, friend, husband, dad and brother. But now you only have one identity: 'police officer'. Your friends don't understand what you have seen, heard and experienced, but your work friends do. As you invest in your new role, you commit yourself heavily to work, you work overtime and socialise with just police staff. Your other life takes a strain, you're not in balance. When did you last talk to your partner? When did you last feel totally at ease? The investment in your police role begins to take more time. Court appearances, training courses, secondments, special events and overtime suck you into more investment. You don't control your time and career, public demand, events, court appearances and administrators control your life. With your police role effectively being taken over, your sense of self and ultimate control becomes fragile. Decisions that are made affect your future plans and lifestyle. You begin to think and feel that injustice is rife within the service, but its rawness is magnified as your sense of self is being threatened. You become resentful of the organisation, blaming management for not caring or listening. You are resentful as management seem to have more control than you do. A huge rift exists between managers and staff. As you stay on the frontline, background stress begins to build, you see incompetent officers rise within the ranks and you ask yourself why you aren't getting promoted? As the years take their toll, you fantasise about retirement and can't wait to get out of the job. It was a job that you loved, that you put your life on the line for and now you go to work hating it every day. It is control that police officers perceive that causes unnecessary problems and can add to the overall problem. Police officers begin to take the role of a victim, a person who has no control over their future destiny.

Dr Kevin M. Gilmartin advises police officers to step away from the overinvestment in the police role. His book suggests that the police job is highly controlling, offers little spontaneity and wrecks havoc with police officers' social lives. It is recommended to aggressively time manage lifestyle pursuits with those nearest and dearest, so that you can claw back control within your personal life. He advises to set out your off duty life with military precision making sure that you visit family and friends, old acquaintances, hobbies, learning, relaxation and physical fitness.

4

PSYCHOLOGICAL STRESS AND ITS SOLUTION

Emotional police work

The clash of ideas, values and our sense of justice happens day by day and adds to a subtle form of procrastination and frustration. The values that an officer holds and his/her sense of justice continually changes. It is not a fixed mindset. We are constantly clashing with our own set of values, because, moment by moment, we are seeing and experiencing traumatic or unsatisfactory events. Domestic violence is a day-to-day example that continually challenges our attitudes.

PC John recalls: "Today I have attended a violent home. The female victim looks depressed, her children are unhappy and her life is a mess. The victim has a bruised face and a large red and swollen strangulation mark around her neck. We have arrested her abuser and he is blaming everyone but himself. After all our efforts, the victim is so shell shocked, broken, stressed and depressed. She doesn't have the strength to talk or provide a statement. She will not assist in the investigation. I was thinking how absolutely terrible, this is awful, those children are seeing mum being degraded and mum is really depressed. **I really want** justice for this woman, **I don't want** her to suffer, she really does need to make a complaint."

She isn't strong enough to make a complaint, that's the reality of this scenario and without other corroborating evidence the abuser isn't charged with an offence. The cycle continues.

PC Johns says: "I know that having observed this family, something is fundamentally wrong. My sense of justice is strong, but I am powerless; with all the training in the world, I have made no difference. I know that we will be back at the same home in a couple of months. My values are strengthened by my inner wanting. **I want justice** for this despicable crime, but at this moment in time, justice is not administered. It is times like these that I think and feel let down by the system."

This is what I am calling 'values frustration'. Our sense of beliefs and values is the exact opposite of what I am observing. "I know that what I am experiencing is fundamentally wrong and that I can do something that can change the series of events." This is an assumption we sometimes believe that we have some power to shape the world as we would like it to be. The police officer is judging the situation based on his/her set of standards. There is no solution to this problem at this time and a narrow, unhelpful mindset can develop. Police officers solve problems every day, but here there is no solution. We are goal driven, as police officers we are seeking a solution. So what really happens? We get very frustrated and, depending on our personal coping strategies, this may further advance anger, hostility, denial or the cold shoulder.

Why?

The answer to this question relates to the emotional response of the individual officer. For instance, because the officer is experiencing 'values frustration', the conditioned response learnt from childhood could be related to 'feeling angry' or 'feeling hopeless'. As a child, if you didn't get your own way (I want), how did you react? Did you sulk or throw a tantrum? Therefore, because of this internal frustration, the officer may be taking on and projecting feelings of anger or other negative states of mind.

Feelings of anger are not pleasant feelings. Nobody is ever happy in anger. Also with such feelings there may be some further link to previous negative experiences. The answer to why officers offer little support is simple. Nobody wants to experience negative states of mind and our normal coping mechanism is the simple act of aversion, or better known as 'denial'. Aversion in its mental capacity can and will translate into unwholesome behaviour and, over time, a reduction of a helping service. Does the question, why do I bother, spring to mind?

The next time we see the same set of circumstances, depending on our state of mind at that time, we may collude with the victim or suspect. This type of collusion will be obvious. Offering no advice, no referral to an appropriate agency and negative body language will be unhelpful. The officer won't listen or support. This process happens to all officers. Continual exposure can pave the way for habits to form. A poor service can be habitual and it is closely linked to the inner experience of values frustration. The only way to address our thinking patterns involves being consciously aware of our own aversive thinking patterns and our own inner feelings. Our internal shift changes from "I want this to happen, I will make this happen" to "I am watching and observing". In essence, our relationship to the result changes and we experience no internal frustration. We are still helping, but we are not drawn into the event from an emotional standpoint. This is also called 'detached acceptance'. Instead of 'imposing' we shift to 'supporting'.

PC Jason recalls one of policing's great lessons:

"It's a busy Saturday night shift and I have been sent out on patrol with my tutor constable. I have been in the job for ten weeks and it's getting tough. We were directed to walk around the town centre. I put on all my kit and I walked with apprehension around the streets.

"I could sense the feeling in the air; it was as if people were over excited and highly anxious. The heat does something to people, nobody was smiling or saying hello. Revellers were bowing their heads and staring at one another. They were on a mission. I could hear the raised voices of people shouting; drunk people normally talk at a very high volume and jeer at anything remotely funny. I was aware of the searing evening heat. I was perspiring and the evening sun was still aggravating my skin. Walking was difficult.

"I could smell the waft of kebab meat, mixed with the sweet fragrance of ladies' perfume; this was a smell I was starting to get used to. I could see groups of males walking to and from pubs. The body language wasn't peaceful and relaxed. Cold stares were being exhibited across the street. Arms pumped up, chest inflated. Hypervigilance and threat surveillance was the method of observation. People were anxious. The conversation was short and sharp. The 'boom boom' of the nightclub music systems played all night. People weren't dancing, they were stamping the floor with the rhythm of the beat. They were preparing for war. I was anxious, nervous and at a time frightened of the unknown.

"My tutor commented: 'Our perceptions of sense (sight, touch, hearing, taste, smell and inner feeling) need to be levelled and balanced on a daily basis. Our senses are our inner doors to listening and observing. You have identified that although nothing has happened yet, the potential for further problems exists.'

"We were directed by a CCTV operator to investigate the suspicious activity of a group of youths. We took a short walk and from a distance of 30m I could see four males huddling around the corner. I approached the males and asked, 'What are you doing?' The males turned around and the more confident leader stepped forward and said, 'Nothing, it's a free country'.

"I thought to myself, 'That's a defensive reaction'. I thought to myself, 'Obviously he is lying, on that basis I think I will search him'.

"I said, 'Right then, Sonny Jim, turn around and place your hands behind your back' and I then grabbed hold of his arms and handcuffed him. The shock and horror on his mates' faces was unbelievable. I thought to myself, 'That will teach him, bloody students'.

"The male started to thrash and resist, and stamp his feet on the floor. The male started to shout, 'I haven't done anything wrong!' A passerby started to look at us. I began to search him and sensed that I would find some drugs, he was the druggie type. Nothing. I undid his handcuffs. The male immediately turned on me and pointed his finger at me. This I really don't like, especially from a 'student'.

"The male said, 'You fucking coppers are all the same'. His face was red, his jaw line tense and chest inflated. He said, "'I want your name and number' and he repeated the same words over and over again. The male then took out of his pocket his mobile phone. He then began to take photographs of me and my colleague. I felt threatened and I couldn't understand why he was behaving so defensively, he was only being searched.

"The male then said, 'I'll take you to the fucking cleaners'. I was enraged by this comment, how dare he say that! I am not tolerating this repugnant male, 'I am arresting you for breaching the Queen's peace'.

"The male was then escorted to the police station. Meanwhile, after the male was released, my tutor gave me a shock debrief. 'Prior to seeing those males, you identified that you were feeling anxious, the information presented to you was from a third party, the CCTV operator. Did it pass your mind that the operator's perception could be clouding his/her judgement?

'We approached the males and, based on a small amount of information, you decided to search the leading male, you controlled him and found nothing. Following this, his behaviour changed and you stepped up your behaviour and arrested him.

'Your skills of observation were poor, remember smell, touch, sight, hearing, feeling.

'Could you smell alcohol or drugs?

'Was the male slurring his speech or talking fast?

'Was the male's body language evasive?

'Was he concealing anything?

'Was his story or account making sense?

'What were his feelings towards you? What were your feelings towards him?

'Once you have the information, then make an ethical decision. From the point of information (smell, touch, sight, hearing, feeling), the next stage of processing begins. The world of inner process dictates our emotional and ethical decision.

'Depending on our past conditioning to responses of ridicule, threat and violence our inner response will be dictated by our thoughts and attitudes, this will effectively change our behaviour.

'You believe that police officers are effectively strong and must never back down.

'You believe that students are lazy and need to get a proper job.

'You believe that students take drugs and are the route of anti-social behaviour.

'Your beliefs are somewhat hardwired based on your past experiences. It is very difficult to consider your beliefs on the spot.

'Your entire being has developed an emotional response to such an event. Your inner feelings will register in three distinct ways:

1. Feelings that you don't like (aversion and denial)

2. Feelings that have no effect whatsoever (in difference)

3. Feelings that you like (enjoyment).

'The dilemma that you faced today was that of a feeling of aversion. Nobody caused you to feel aversion, you are the creator of your own response your own inner world. The reality of that arrest, shows that both of your behaviours affected one another, you were connected in some way. You are now in a different position to the student, because you have power and influence.

'If you're honest with yourself, you felt frustrated and you projected those feelings into action. You took away his liberty because you were feeling discomfort within your own heart.

'The concept of "I" develops; "I don't like students". Now the idea of "me" arises. Once the sense of "I" has developed, certain feelings will register.

'You may feel a tightening towards the chest, heaviness in the forehead and greater dislike for what you are experiencing. Your body language changed and your shoulders started to tense.

'The reaction to such feeling is an empowerment towards action. "I" must do something. You decided to arrest that person. Actions will translate into three distinct overlapping phases:

1. Negative and prolonged thinking (anger, frustration, hatred)

2. Physical action (physicality, control)

3. Verbal action (sarcasm, put downs, neglect, ridicule).'

Everything – from the reception of the word at the ear or sight of the male standing – has been an internal process dependent on our own conditioning. In this case, the student officer conditioned a response of 'angry response'. The continued response causes mental and physical turbulence.

Recognising the effects of aversion in the police service

Aversion

The officer may avoid dealing with such crime reports in a sympathetic manner, the officer's attention to detail may wane. Commonly, officers may say "It's only a domestic", "We can't prove this one, so let's not record it", "Why bother, nobody does anything". This is a defence mechanism and serves to minimise the suffering of the officer witnesses.

The officer may avoid work at all costs, avoid answering calls, avoid assisting colleagues, avoid team working. The officer may also look for the easy performance indicator. Arresting someone on a warrant or actively putting themselves forward for the easier task. Working with a highly aversive officer can be demoralising. If they are a highly influential character they may sway the team to constantly thinking negatively or convincing people that the job is not worth doing.

Aversive officers constantly move around looking for a new role, they feel the

need to escape. They may also become experts in their field furthering a defensive position. This expert status is a safety net and will give them a whole host of reasons not to do a particular task. "Sorry that's not in my remit", "Policy says I can't do this or that". Aversive individuals hide behind the organisation.

On the same continuum of aversion is that of annihilation. The officer may start to engage in dangerous situations. For example, throwing themselves into a large-scale fight and not caring about the consequences; driving far too fast; frequent and heavy alcohol consumption; taking prescription drugs or illegal substances. Recklessness can have dire consequences.

Blame shifting

Because the result is negative, the officer may blame a fellow colleague, a neighbouring department or even an outside agency. How many times have you heard officers criticise the legal profession or the local social services department? Projection of negative feelings is very common. The officer will blame and offer no personal ownership for a particular problem.

Blame shifting can cause huge communication problems between departments. "I thought you were going to do it." Assumptions about work allocation can lead to the task not being completed. Blame shifting creates an unhealthy working environment. Staff are almost 'treading on egg shells', asking officers what mood is he or she exhibiting. We all have our particular supervisors and colleagues whom we choose to avoid. They are so predictable and it can be a real headache getting something past them.

Feeling a failure

Common thoughts include:

"This child has suffered because of me. I am to blame, I am a failure." This is quite a common feature within individuals who are caring and show high levels of empathy.

The nature of police work is seeing and experiencing unsatisfactory and challenging experiences. Police officers encounter whole strata of experiences that create the causes of severe 'values frustration'. Hopelessness is a feature that can take us down the river of frustration and depression. When an officer interprets a policing experience into a personal failure it is somewhat over exaggerated. The experience can register feelings of failure, despair and guilt.

For example: an officer may have been abused as a child. The officer as a child would have experienced feelings of fear, guilt and pain. The officer's past experiences and emotional memory will serve to memorise them when attending disturbing domestic abuse and child neglect calls. Whenever an officer comes into contact with a negative experience that has some personal meaning, the suffering of the victim can be shared by the officer. This is also known as 'taking on the suffering of others'. This process is a huge personal burden that officers take on.

Our past and present experiences shape our reactions to our day-to-day policing experiences. We cannot ignore that cause and effect is operating within the hearts and minds of police officers the world over. Police officers witness, observe, involve and immerse themselves in human pain and suffering. This effect of immersion creates the causes for our own adverse morale problems. For as long as we are police officers, we will continue to be affected by negative states of mind. 'We are a mirror of our experience.'

Negative states of mind rule us at our very being; we are clearly a product of the society that we are observing. Even though we are at far greater vulnerability to depressing circumstances. We do have some say in the way in which we think, behave, act and engage with this world. However, it is my belief that because of the special circumstances that we are part of, the police service must make it a daily priority to consider, help and support those miraculous officers. The service must proactively seek to make the working conditions conducive to healthy morale.

Counteracting the threat of the ruminating mind

The radio operator informs us that a call needs to be attended to. "Can a unit attend a call to assist a member of the public, Mrs Loveluck hasn't seen her neighbour for a number of days and she can see mail stacked up in the hallway and there are milk bottles on the doorstep?" Sound familiar? What are you thinking? If you are thinking about death, you're probably right. So you go to the filing cabinet and pick up the relevant form, you briefly rememorize the sudden death procedures, pick up your Vaseline, gloves and torch. The body tags are in your briefcase. Still, the thought of death registers, your heart sinks. Images of blue bottles and grieving relatives fill your mind. Your heart sinks deeper and you feel slightly upset. Push those thoughts back, you tell yourself, push them back, it will be OK. But you know it won't be OK, the family will be crying, even blaming you. As you walk to the patrol car, trudging along, your inner critic says, "I hate this job". As you drive to the location getting closer, the thoughts and feelings of DEATH, DEATH, DEATH get amplified. Are you felling happy at this moment in time? You arrive at the location and speak to the neighbour. Mrs Loveluck explains that she doesn't know her neighbour very well and fears the worst. You knock on the door, no answer. You look through the windows, expecting the worse. All of a sudden, by chance, a car stops and the local postman identifies himself. The postman says, "You won't get much answer, he has gone to Thailand on holiday". Phew, thank heavens for that. The neighbour looks at you with bewilderment. It is one of those looks that is quite disappointed, a feeling of not being the town gossip. The call is updated and you go on your way to the next tragedy.

Ask yourself some questions? The thoughts and feelings that you experienced prior to attending the call, were they based on reality? Did your thoughts and feelings help the situation? When you were immersed in worrying mode, were you consciously aware of what you were actually doing? Did assumption overtake present moment awareness? Rumination is a process of being trapped, a process of re-cycling worrying thoughts and magnifying the emotional response. It is somewhat difficult to break this habit, when as a police officer you constantly predict doom and a final outcome. Rumination is a heavy burden and can hinder the opportunities to look at crime in a more balanced perspective. When we harbour inner thinking patterns, we blind ourselves to what we are actually seeing. The officer was expecting to see a dead body lying on the floor, but saw nothing. It is this process of expectation that can get in the way of actually seeing and experiencing. If our minds are filled with 'other' thoughts, we are occupied and cannot see and experience clearly. A police officer's job is to investigate using the full faculty of awareness and act as a witness, but this is hampered because of the ruminating mind. The ruminating mind is not in the here and now, it is a state of mind that is in its own virtual reality.

Values frustration can change from minute to minute, due to the unpredictability of the police service. There are certain times of your working year that can predict the likelihood of values frustration being stronger or weaker. An example of a strong frustrated response would be the officer working over the Christmas period. Christmas is a time of giving, goodwill and joy to many. A time when domestic violence peaks and family arguments fester, a time when police officers work very hard indeed. Think back over the years and consider times of severe frustration. You may be able to identify a pattern of frustration. Identifying a pattern may give you the opportunity to strengthen your own coping skills or work-life balance.

Mastering emotional responses the use of mindfulness meditation

What is policing?

I am going to present a different view of what policing is. When we join the service we can be bamboozled by policing talk. We hear slogans that serve to confuse us: "citizen focus", "neighbourhood engagement" etc. But what really is policing?

To consider what we are doing is a profound realisation. We are all different in needs, temperaments and philosophies. For me, and you don't have to agree, the public have taught me a great deal. I soon realised that people commit criminal acts because of deep-seated habitual states of mind.

An abusive partner may assault his partner because of control hatred and jealousy. A drug addict may commit a burglary because of a deep-seated need and attachment to hard drugs. A mental health patient may injure someone due to hearing voices in their head. A prolific criminal may commit crime because they may not have any other livelihood. Crime is co-dependent on the offender's current mindset. States of mind are dependent on numerous internal and external factors. For me, anger, jealousy, retaliation, hatred, malice, attachment, greed and lack of empathy are the real criminals.

I thought long and hard to come up with a real world idea, and it dawned on me one day; we 'observe'. Yes, that's right, we get paid to sit and watch, listen and observe the misfortune, suffering and unsatisfactory life of our communities. We've got the best CV for the job, road traffic accidents, child abuse, domestic violence, hate crime, murder, bullying, town centre disorder, suicide, distraction burglary etc.

Putting observation one step further, we are 'ethical observers'. Don't confuse ethics with right and wrong, you will only get confused. We observe people's mental, physical and emotional suffering and dissatisfaction. The ethical term relates to our legal powers and our willingness to listen, act and make the intention to help.

Day by day we see, perceive and listen to some horrendous stories. My old Inspector used to say, "If it feels wrong, then there is probably a law that says it is". What he was referring to was this observation within us all. An old colleague of mine, a 30-year beat man Lyn Ingram, used to start the shift every day by sitting by the window for about 10 minutes. I asked him one day what he was doing He replied, "I have had some of my best arrests because I sat and watched". Little did I realise he was teaching me the absolute skill that all professionals possess, the art of 'external watching'.

What separates those great police officers that you work with from the rest? You know the ones that can smell crime, always find a drink driver, catch a drug dealer or trip a burglar up in an interview. I have had the good fortune to work with some excellent police officers and, for me, it is that 'confidence in awareness' that sets them apart. You can train officers in all the technicalities and they can write policies blindfolded, but there is nothing that impresses me more than people who have awareness. Can this awareness be achieved by everyone? What is this awareness and how does it link to stress reduction? The answer to this question is the practice of mindfulness meditation.

Mindfulness Meditation is the practice of inner observation. As I outlined earlier, police officers are 'ethical observers' in the realm of the external world. The world external to us and all its tragedy has a relationship with our mind and body. We are immersed in human suffering and it affects us. Meditation is simply an inner investigative process of literally paying attention to inner feelings, thoughts, body sensations, touch, taste and smell. By turning inwards we are allowing ourselves to process, manage and make sense of what we are seeing and perceiving. We are allowing calm and relaxation to pervade our senses at any giving moment.

The research evidence

Mindfulness Meditation has been scientifically tested and the results of the programme are validated and profound. Over 100 studies have been conducted. Recently, American Special Forces used the mindfulness technique prior to being deployed in a war-time operation. Special Forces operatives reported and concluded that memory and concentration improved. Studies have been conducted in workplaces and have shown to improve morale and decrease stress. Mindfulness Meditation has shown to lower cardiac risk factors pertaining to heart disease, reduce the prevalence of depression and anxiety. Mindfulness Meditation has shown to improve morale and reduce burnout in A&E physicians. In California, schools are using the programme to de-stress students and the results have shown to improve students' behaviour and improve concentration and learning outcomes. The application of this cheap and easy technique has many policing implications, from stress reduction, to operational decision making, to training and morale issues.

Values frustration is the reason why police officers' patterns of negative thinking repeat over and over like a broken record player. This re-living and re-experiencing emotional agitation and frustration is a major source of stress and leaves us feeling exhausted and unable to cope. We become apathetic and feel our life energy draining away. This finding was the main cause of stress in a study of 3,000+ Norwegian Police Officers.

Anxiety and stress has an internal structure in the form of habitual cognitive reactions to which we have become blindly attached through the process of identification. The negative thought arises and then we become the thought. A worry-thought arises and we become worried. Anger arises and we become angry. Fear arises and we become afraid. This process of becoming happens quite automatically and is sustained by the fact that we are unaware of the reactive process of becoming. The thought arises and literally grabs hold of us and pulls us into a predetermined state of consciousness against our will or choice. Habitual reactions thrive on our unawareness of them and will continue indefinitely so long as we remain unaware. So, clearly, the very first step in overcoming values frustration requires that we reverse this process and train ourselves to become aware of our negative emotional reactions. As the saying goes, 'no consciousness, no choice; partial consciousness, partial choice; complete consciousness, complete choice'.

We may think that we are aware of our thoughts and emotions, and this is true up to a point, but the issue is that we are seldom aware of our reactions in the moment that they arise, only after the fact when we are consumed by becoming the reaction. Our awareness is not immediate and direct, but delayed, and the delaying factor is unawareness. Mindfulness is first and foremost a deliberate effort to change this and awaken to our reactions as soon as they arise. In fact, we learn to recognise the impulse to react that precedes the thought form itself. Each moment in which we become mindful of our impulse to react creates a space, a brief interval in which there is freedom and choice. Sometimes this is all it takes to interrupt the reactive process altogether and we are able to choose to think or act differently. Other times, the impulse is so strong that we are tempted back into becoming the reaction again. Nevertheless, each moment of mindfulness strengthens and cultivates this inner state of freedom and with conscious effort and repetition, the space of inner freedom will grow. What we are learning to do is to refrain from feeding the beast, the inner structure of habitual reactivity. If you stop feeding a reaction by becoming identified by it then it will begin to lose power to sustain itself. It will also lose its power over you.

Now that you have gained some freedom from your reactivity, you can do something quite remarkable and actively turn your attention towards the suffering, towards the feeling energy that fuels the impulse to react.

When we are in the unaware reactive mode of consciousness, we do anything but turn towards our pain. We react further to the anxiety, fear or depression with secondary reactions of avoidance, resistance and aversion. We seek positive distractions; we try to drown our sorrows in drink, obsessive sensory stimulation, or work. We become aggressive and project our inner suffering onto others and even onto those we love. But, through mindfulness, we are able to avoid the secondary reactions of aversion, wanting and distraction and come back to the simple process of being present with our frustration. You may think you are present for it, but if you look more closely you will probably see that you are not really present, but reactive. Even the act of thinking about why you are upset or worried is NOT the same as being fully present for the feeling. Interestingly, police officers who are aversive are more likely to experience stress and work absenteeism. Mindfulness is the art of being awake to every subtle movement of mind that tries to take you away from being present.

In the example of the probationer police officer, he just reacted blindly to his thoughts and feelings about the person in front of him. This culminated in an unlawful arrest and subsequent inner frustration.

So, through the practice of mindfulness, we learn to be more and more present with our experience, including our direct experience of inner frustration. This has a remarkable effect on the configuration of emotional energy attached to the negative thought or belief. The feeling energy begins to regain mobility and malleability and, in the inner free space of mindful-awareness, the emotion begins to change. An emotion is an unstable configuration of energy, and the psych will always seek to resolve instability as long as it has the freedom to change. Mindfulness creates this inner freedom and this is why mindfulness is so therapeutic. As we say, 'reactivity sustains suffering; mindfulness resolves suffering'. We do not have to try and change the suffering; it changes itself – as long as we stay mindful.

This book, although an advocate for the practice of mindfulness meditation, advises to seek a suitably qualified teacher of mindfulness meditation. There are a number of good books and CDs that can be used as an introduction to this practice; however, a suitable course over eight weeks is highly recommended. Jon Kabat-Zinn has written an excellent book 'Full Catastrophe Living' and has produced a number of CDs (available from www.mindfulnesstapes.com).

Body awareness

The ability to recognise how your body reacts to stress can be the start of responding to stress and not reacting. When we wake in the morning, we pay attention to the weather, our feelings of sleepiness and our general day-to-day to-do list. We don't consider tension within the body. Our body registers stress long before the conscious mind does. Muscle tension is the body's first internal signpost that stress is taking hold. Body awareness is the first step to acknowledging and reducing stress. You inevitably tense your body when you experience stress and whilst removing tension will act to remove stress. Making the differentiation between the external and internal world of awareness is an important step to seeing stress for what it actually is. External awareness includes the stimulation from the five senses. Internal awareness refers to any physical sensation, feeling or emotional discomfort. Much of the tension within the body isn't experienced because most of your awareness is directed toward the outside world.

Try the following exercise:

- ❏ Focus your attention on the outside world, start sentences like, "I am aware of…", consciously bring every day events into your awareness.

- ❏ After you have become aware of everything that is going on around you, shift to focusing your attention on your body and your physical sensations. Start sensations like "I am aware of feeling warm, tension in my neck" etc.

- ❏ Move between your inner and outer worlds. When you feel stressed or defensive, notice your inner reactions and how your inner world changes as a result of the outer world. Notice your reaction, how long does this experience stay, does it go somewhere?

- ❏ Write about your experiences and splurge them onto a page.

Body scanning

Lie down or sit up, adopt a comfortable position based on your own needs.

Close your eyes. Starting with your toes and moving up your body, ask yourself "Where am I tense?" When you find a tense part of your body, try to place focused attention towards the area. What does it feel like? Is the tension painful? Is the tension moving or stationary? Focus on your breathing, feel the inhale of your breath and feel the rib cage expand, relax and exhale. Breathe naturally, allowing a passive attention to develop. Allow your body scan to move inch by inch along the body. Are there parts of the body that you cannot feel? Is there tension in one side of the body? As you exhale, say to yourself "I am letting go of tension, this feeling is as it should be".

Breathing

Lie down on a blanket on the floor. Bend your knees and move your feet about eight inches apart, with your toes turned slightly outward. Settle into a relaxing natural curvature of the spine.

Scan your body for tension. Place one hand on your abdomen and one hand on your chest. Inhale slowly and deeply through your nose and into your abdomen to push up your hand as much as feels comfortable. Exhale slowly through your mouth. Focus on the feeling of breathing as you become more relaxed. Continue to breathe deeply for five to ten minutes and continue to increase your relaxation time each week. When you become accustomed to this technique, introduce deep breathing at times when you feel uptight and stressed.

Mindfulness meditation

Meditation is the practice of focusing one's attention on one meditation object at any one time. Different techniques use varying different objects, such as a candle, symbol, sound, mantra or breath. The nature of the mind is that it continually wants to undermine and move from thought to thought. In meditation, we are not trying to rigidly control our thoughts. Our experience is more to do with observing thoughts, feelings and body sensations and returning our awareness to the mediation object. We need to be gentle, apply gentle effort, gentle concentration. Much of our stress comes from worrying about the past or the future. In a policing sense, worry can dominate our decision-making processes and we sometimes miss what is happening right now, under our nose. When we notice our mind wandering towards thoughts of the future and the past, we note this process and focus our attention to the present moment. Mindfulness accepts the here and now, even if the here and now is somewhat turbulent, we don't fight against these inner turbulences and accept them for what they are.

For example, in a policing context, you may be at an incident where someone is being abusive and says "All cops are corrupt and take bribes". This type of insult is common and the person continues to shout and repeat his mantra. Feeling uptight and annoyed, your actions may translate into anger and retaliation. The meditator would hear those words "All cops are corrupt and take bribes" and observe the inner feeling of 'getting frustrated'. The meditator would then label this turbulence as the inner voice as 'feeling, feeling'. The deep breathing exercise would also coincide with this mental noting. The police officer is making a distinction between the inner and outer worlds. Making this clear distinction gives us choice in responding and not reacting with anger or hostility.

There are many different techniques to choose from including eating, walking and breathing meditation. The website **www.bemindfulonline.com** has created an excellent online course. The course has been validated and has been proven to reduce stress and anxiety.

Visualisation

The power of our minds can create the cause of peace and joy. Our own minds can become a refuge of tranquillity, safety, warmth, love and security. Create your own special place that mixes positive aromas, colour, feeling and sound. Fill your place with sensuous detail; create a mid-ground, foreground and background.

My personal visualisation includes catching the perfect wave:

"Standing on the shore, the sun slowly rises in the East, I can feel the cool sand surround my feet as I move slowly through the powder-like sand, the warmth of the new day's sun radiates on my face. The quiet shore break lapping onto the beach, silence and calmness. I am alone; my heart is open to the new day, patient, kind, gentle and accepting. Nature surrounds me, birds singing, a seal playing in the ocean. The waves perfectly formed, forming a gold band of reflection across the sea. I sit on my surfboard and paddle out across the unbroken waves, aware of my breath, slow and deep, I am relaxed. A wave forms, I paddle and rise to my feet with effortless ease. Slowly, feeling the power of Mother Nature below, I turn my surfboard and see the line of the shoulder. The deep dark opportunity presents itself, I crouch and hold, I am inside the barrel, power and time stand still, energy rushing through every cell within my body. I escape, I am reborn, I am high, I am perfection, I just got tubed!"

The golden view of policing is a view that is observational and independent, we observe society, we have very little control over the public's willingness to engage in destruction. There may be radio broadcasts and posters on the wall, telling people to curb alcohol-related violence, but across every town in every part of the UK, someone, somewhere is getting assaulted. Everywhere we look with our 'police eyes' someone, somewhere is committing and indulging in destructive and unwholesome behaviour. There isn't a moment across the whole world where everyone is at peace. What has this philosophy got to do with time management? The position that I stand from is one of flexibility. Once there is a shift to accepting that we have moderately little control over our policing time, we can accept that our use of time is also dependent on other factors beyond our control. We could have the best team of officers and a highly organised department, but it only takes one member of the public to act in anger and hostility for five seconds and your plans for the week, or even the month, could effectively be turned upside down. On the other end of the continuum, we have sometimes moderate control, when we can make decisions and our decision-making process can and will affect our time and attention in the future. **Sometimes you do not have control over time.** One of the ways to overcome this issue, is to ask for time protection. This is a time when you are sidelined for the entire day and given the time to concentrate on your workload, without the demands of the radio or the public.

Mindfulness and time

By being aware of our every timely action, we will be able to identify the parts of the working day, when our concentration wanes, times when we daydream, gossip, work and procrastinate. If we use our pocket notebooks as a time marker, we will be able to identify how we use our time. If we look over our work over a period of a week, we will be able to identify a pattern of ebb and flow. Our working spirit dips and falls just as our body changes. There are times of the working week when it's probably not the best time to start planning a new project, conversely taking a detailed statement is also a matter of timing. Our policing culture is goal-driven and it can become confusing as to what is a priority and what is not. Every department has a policy that dictates timeliness. For example, domestic violence reports have to be completed within a 24-hour period, similar timelines exist with regard to submitting road traffic accident reports. Ask yourself a question. **By not acting in a timely manner, am I putting someone at risk from harm or abuse?** This single question should prompt you to consider what is important and what is not.

Traditionally the workplace will use a goal-setting approach to the use of time and being able to achieve work objectives. This type of approach, although having some merits, may not be the best approach for police officers. Having a rigid goal approach and not achieving goals, because of policing demands, may de-motivate you. Instead of having goals, consider your approach as 'work in progress', the work will get done, but at the moment there are reasons why it isn't getting done. Always record those reasons. The following headings may serve to benefit you.

Instead of asking the question 'Will I be criticised if I don't attend to this incident?', a defensive standpoint, ask the following questions:

- ❏ Will further physical harm come to this person if I don't act now?

- ❏ If I don't act now, will this incident create further demand for me and my colleagues? A proactive standpoint.

The first question determines if an incident is URGENT and the second question determines if an incident is IMPORTANT.

Important	Urgent
Important	Not Urgent
Not Important	Urgent
Not Important	Not Urgent

Once the incident has been identified as URGENT and IMPORTANT we really need to begin to understand the needs, concerns and expectations of the persons involved in the incident. The police service traditionally has a policy that covers what needs to be done. This sometimes can create even more work, when by actually identifying the person's needs we can match those needs with the appropriate resource and partnership agency.

Needs	**Referrals to**
Emotional support	Counselling / Samaritans
Crime prevention advice	Specialist Crime Prevention Officer
Language	Interpreters
Cultural needs	Advice from Specialist Persons
Understanding the legal system	Referral to an online presentation
Police procedure	Detailed explanation

Needs	**Referrals to**
Ownership	OIC identified
Specialists	

Concerns

Communication

Retaliation

Press / Gossip

Expectations

The boomerang effect

You would have noticed how work keeps coming back to you. After completing a file of evidence, you take a sigh of relief, only to be reminded that the work hasn't finished, as a full file of evidence is required some six weeks later. The CPS send a memo with a number of outstanding actions, statements to take and enquiries to be made. In the police office, other departments contact you because you haven't filled in the correct form and submitted the correct paperwork within the appropriate timescales.

Identify within your place of work the activities that come back and require more attention and detail. These activities are telling you something, you must invest more time and effort at the very start of these activities. The golden hour is a term used by investigators that seeks to improve the quality of an investigation. The first few moments of a crime being committed are crucial and it's within the first hour that crimes are solved. Energy and focus within the 'golden hour' will save countless hours of further statements and enquiries. By seizing the initiative and getting as much detail as possible, you create the very likely conditions that an offender will admit guilt and a guilty plea will be entered at court. This will serve to reduce additional paperwork and cut attendance at court proceedings. We all know that the courts don't care about our days off. **The golden hour is what it says it is. Remind yourself that every action has an equal and opposite reaction.**

Deadlines

The use of this word isn't positive and creates an absolute, fixed and unmovable standpoint. Agreement lines are a far better description. Usually paperwork is set by administrators, who may not understand the finer aspects of police work. Administrators may not have any knowledge of your current demands and it can appear to be infuriating when we receive a memo with 'VERY URGENT DEADLINE' written in red ink. Old-fashioned school teachers always marked poor work in red ink. Administrators who are behind the scenes can be your best friend or your worst enemy. Before you start in a station, make the time to meet them and offer them a cup of tea and a biscuit. Take an interest in your background staff, you would be amazed how much difference this will make. Above all, talk and communicate, explain that the current deadline is unachievable because of x, y and z. Co-operate with background support staff.

The 20 / 80 rule

Vilfredo Pareto, an Italian economist, noted that 20 percent of what we do, yields 80 percent of the results. Conversely, 80 percent of what we do, yields 20 percent of the results. This principle can be applied to police work. In a typical day, we are called to help the public in a range of different ways, from legal advice to crime prevention. Identify the caller's needs and supporting them from a needs perspective is what good police work looks like.

If the victim wants someone to talk to, advise them to ring the Samaritans or victim support. If they want crime prevention advice, tell them to visit the internet and watch 'How to' videos on YouTube. If a victim requires further support, refer them to a befriending service or counselling agency. So much of what the police do and listen to doesn't require our intervention. Other agencies are the key to matching needs and improving the response. The public are looking to you for guidance.

In the majority of cases, other agencies will be more appropriate, but there is sometimes fear from the bottom ranks that delegation is avoiding work. This is not the case, it's just working smarter. By identifying a range of agencies within your area of work, you will be able to cut the amount of time that you give to people, ensuring that needs are met and satisfactions levels increase. **Work smart, remember the 20/80 rule.**

Minimise and maximise time wasters

Avoid telephone interruptions, unproductive meetings and briefings, and learn to say no to others. Cut down on spending time with people who don't require your time. However, if you are engaged in crime scene duties or sitting at a pre- planned event, use this down time to organise, plan, email, review and communicate with your audience.

Talk talk

When planning and arranging your workload, explain to your audience that police work is sometimes beyond your control. For instance, if you are due to take a statement from a witness, say "I will try to be at your home at 2pm, but please be advised that police work is changeable and I might be late, it is not because I am ignoring you". Ring your audience in advance and explain that things are going wrong. **Communicate all the time and reinforce the message that there needs to be flexibility from both sides.**

One job at a time

Focus your attention on one activity in any given moment. This can be done as long as you plan your day and allow for a degree of flexibility. When you receive a distraction such as the radio or a new task, slowly and deliberately, pause, breathe and move onto the next task. Expect distractions, but don't react with frustration. This is where the practice of mindfulness can really help those daily distractions. Purchase a diary and plan your week according to your current demands. Prioritise your day into the following areas:

Work demands – What activities need to be completed today? What activities are going to come back to me? How do I prevent this? What activities serve to protect the public?

Rest and refreshments – What time will be best for food?

Improving relationships – Who do I need to talk to and improve relationships with?

Planning – What is on the policing horizon, what do I need to plan for? What event is going to take more of my time and effort?

Self-care – How do I feel? How can I improve my own morale?

Communication – Who do I need to tell, that all is not going to plan?

Procrastination

There are many activities within the policing role that we would rather not do. Make a list of all the unpleasant tasks that you are avoiding and then make a list of all the consequences of putting that task off. Objectively, consider the discomfort of procrastination versus the cost of consequences. Ask yourself which list contains the greater degree of unpleasantness. Start small with your task and ease yourself in gently. Reward yourself as you start to complete and master your task. Give yourself a positive affirmation and be gentle with yourself.

Sometimes you do not have control over time.	Co-operate with background support staff.	One job at a time. Purchase a diary and plan each week loosely.
By not acting in a timely manner, am I putting someone at risk from harm or abuse?	Work smart; remember the 20/80 rule.	Instead of having goals, consider your approach as 'work in progress', the work will get done, but at the moment there are reasons why it isn't getting done.
The golden hour is what it says it is. Remind yourself that every action has an equal and opposite reaction. Seize the opportunity to reduce future demand.	Communicate all the time and reinforce the message that there needs to be flexibility from both sides.	Reward yourself and be gentle with yourself. Partnership working reduces demand.

Thinking about difficult situations - Preparing youself

Family Liaison Officer

This has to be one of the most demanding roles within the police service. I have admiration for the officers who volunteer for this role. I said earlier that policing is about 'observing' and this role is about observing a family's upset, hurt, distress and pain. Words cannot describe the emotional upset that families go through. This role is demanding and can be especially demoralising if the same officer is 'observing and experiencing'. The service has recognised the heaviness that this role can induce and forces train officers to a high standard and offer regular counselling and emotional support.

Death

Death is a subject that we are not meant to talk about, a subject that is misunderstood by many (its fundamental nature is clouded by horror, tragedy and suspicion). We are programmed to avoid this subject, but some professions walk side by side with it every moment of every day. Death to the police officer is like childbirth for midwives. As a frontline officer, you will never escape its grasp. It's not fair, it doesn't discriminate, it has no warning, it doesn't make sense and leaves an impression of a lifetime of feelings; guilt, regret, shame, sadness. However, in other circumstances, it can be a release, a reminder, a message, a turn of a new chapter and the start of something great. Death is certain, life is uncertain.

For the officer, it can be the reminder of past experiences both personal and professional and its long-term exposure can have a long-lasting effect. You may be feeling tired, tired of attending another grieving family. Turn the experience around and focus on the tremendous gift that you have been given. The first moment of holding a newborn child is such a great honour and an important life experience. The beauty, spectacle and miracle that we all are, becomes a profound realisation. We take life for granted, we believe that tomorrow will be, but how do we really know? Standing at the bedside of a dead person, with a large family supporting and loving one another, I have often reflected on how important and special this person was to so many and the real advances that can be made when we make our life meaningful. A person who lives with value and meaning, inspires. A police officer attending many processes of death, can begin to see the final moments and the real benefits of living a peaceful, insightful and tranquil life.

When a great person dies, many people come to pay their respects and offer words of hope and thanks, the opposite is true for a selfish and evil person. Death is a message, we must try harder to live with peace and relate to one another. The next death that you attend, sit back and make your observations, consider the experience in a positive light. Share your experience with your family and consider the value and learning of such an approach.

The police perspective

When attending many teenage suicides, I made the connection between domestic violence, emotional abuse and teenage suicide. I had witnessed warring families and then, almost a decade later, the children of such families began to commit suicide. This insight could not have been made if it wasn't for the police service and its relationship with death. This insight paved the way for a self-help book to be produced and has been given to thousands of families.

Suicide

A frontline officer's most difficult circumstance is undoubtedly suicide. Firstly, breaking the news can be nerve wracking. You just don't know what to expect. Will they faint, cry or start smashing things up? After the shock has set in, families need to gather as much information as possible. This analysis can be difficult, as information may be pieced together from many sources. The facts can be misled and great many theories surface. Theories conflict and families start to blame one another. The funerals can be stressful times for families and can end up as personal battles.

Families are torn apart because of the 'not knowing' that suicide shadows. It's the police officer who is 'piggy in the middle', after witnessing, explaining and supporting the family, it's the police officer who will have to arrest family members for criminal damage, harassment and assault. It is a frustrating process that can fester within families for years.

Bearers of unpleasant news

Speaking to people and knocking on doors is part and parcel of day-to-day police life. It never ceases to stun me how the public make honest statements when we do knock on their doors. Knock, knock "Has something happened, is there something wrong?" says Mrs Smith. With our very first meeting with Joe Public, we are mostly faced with a defensive anticipatory response. It's not surprising that this happens as we seldom bring good news to people. "Hello, just to let you know your neighbours have been burgled" and "Good morning, were you woken last night, your neighbour has been assaulted and is in hospital?"

Looking at our role from a balanced perspective, there is good news that we do feedback to victims, witnesses and communities. This news always involves a proportion of the beginnings of unsatisfactory experience. "Following a drugs death, we have made an arrest and a local man is remanded in custody." When we report positive news, it is never entirely for the absolute benefit of the community, it always has a negative story behind it. Think about it.

If you have worked within a defined community for some time, you will be aware that being the messenger of distressing news can be tiresome and demanding. Sometimes community officers can shoulder the extra burden as 'they know the family'. If you live and work within your home town, you may feel that you cannot escape other people's misfortunes and pain. Simple day-to-day activities can serve to remind you of what you have seen, who you have told. Officers have reported a closing of feelings and emotions, and sharing of pain and grief. This is what is known as 'compassionate burnout'. This form of stress is very real and has to be a consideration for the supervisory officer who has to choose the bearer of bad news.

Targeted

Being judged

It's a strange experience driving around in a police car for the first time. Those strange looks, drivers rapidly apply those unused seatbelts, teenagers looking at the ground or the subtle sneer of hatred from some members of the public. Socially we have restrictions, we are told when we first join not to: go to certain pubs, avoid certain groups, remain impartial, tell senior officers where we want to live, etc. Those restrictions, after time, become choices.

Many police officers don't want to go drinking in town centres or remind themselves of the experiences of the beat. The quiet life is a better option. The paradox of police work is that we are told that we must not judge people. However, in our day-to-day work, we are continually being watched and judged. Think about it (CCTV, the public, peers, supervisors, agencies, the IPCC).

Many people hold rigid preconceived ideas of a police officer, what they do and how they contribute. In the same breath, many police officers hold rigid ideas of the public. Parents make me cringe. Walking along my beat one day, a parent grabbed hold of her toddler and shouted at her. "That police man will lock you up and take you away if you're naughty." If I had a pound for every time I heard those words, I would be rich man. At an early age, children can be seriously misled by their peers. As a police officer, it is always worth reminding yourself that different people hold differing views about you, depending on their experiences. We can be unfairly judged and it can take a very long time before people can trust us. This 'trust' I talk about can also be translated as 'suspicion'. Unfairly, people judge our actions, we are an easy target. You may feel sometimes that you are banging your head against a brick wall and that no change is possible. There lies another frustration of modern policing. It is a long-term, patient project, a 30-year project!

It is a difficult position to balance, some people by their very disposition sometimes need to be told no. "I am not allowing you to behave or enter this road. We are not having a conversation about this, you will be doing what I say!" There is much investment today about public confidence. By the very nature of police work, we cannot please everyone at all times of the day, but that doesn't excuse us from listening, being honest and explaining that we cannot deliver promises today. It is worth remembering that your actions today will affect the mindset of future generations. Your application of a commonsense style of policing will make a difference to the way in which your future colleagues police and deal with the public. The old village bobby is still talked about today, that's 40 years since he walked his beat. Now that's public respect and confidence. My predecessor, by his style, paved the way for an easy transition, I was readily accepted because of him. I have him to thank for altering the people's mindset. A living legend.

There is no quick fix, no magic formula, it's about morale, and happy, open-minded police officers make the biggest difference in very trying circumstances. The irony is simple, we don't like to be judged and neither do the public. The more we judge, the less we achieve and the more ammunition we give the public to judge us!

CHAPTER SUMMARY

- ❏ Slow down and pace yourself.
- ❏ Observe your policing experiences using the full faculty of awareness.
- ❏ Take time to reflect and pause.
- ❏ Learn how to make use of mindfulness meditation.
- ❏ Identify times of emotional distress be gentle with yourself.

5

GETTING
EXTRA HELP
AND SUPPORT

Online Life Coaching www.livinglifetothefull.com

Living Life to the Full is a life skills course that aims to provide access to high-quality, user-friendly training in practical approaches you can use in your own life.

The course content teaches key knowledge in how to tackle and respond to issues/demands which we all meet in our everyday lives.

Below is an overview of the type of things the course covers:

- ❑ Understanding why we feel as we do.
- ❑ Practical problem-solving skills.
- ❑ Using Anxiety Control Training relaxation.
- ❑ Overcoming reduced activity.
- ❑ Helpful and unhelpful behaviours.
- ❑ Using medication effectively.
- ❑ Noticing unhelpful thoughts.
- ❑ Changing unhelpful thoughts.
- ❑ Healthy living – sleep, food, diet and exercise.
- ❑ Staying well.

What would you like to get out of the course?

- ❑ We all need life skills in our work, relationships and in every other aspect of our lives.

- ❑ Probably, we all have very different reasons for doing the course:
  - some of us may suffer or are suffering from depression/anxiety or distress;
  - some of us may be caring/supporting people who are facing anxiety or depression;
  - some of us may be working with people suffering from anxiety/depression.

Whatever your reason for wanting to learn these life skills, we hope the content proves helpful. The skills taught cover general skills/information we can all use in our lives when we feel under pressure, stressed or distressed.

Course content and materials

- ❑ Sound, text and video clips are used throughout.

- ❑ Free short handouts supplement the course. Longer detailed practical workbooks that develop and build upon the course are available as the Overcoming Depression: Five Areas workbooks.

- ❑ Moderated discussion forums are available to help course users swap ideas, information and provide mutual support.

Remember: Nothing is compulsory – you are in control. After completing the initial registration process and Session 1, you can choose to complete as many or as few of the self-help life skills modules as you wish. You don't have to use or buy anything.

Why self-help as a way of teaching life skills?

Self-help materials are increasingly available and are popular with the general public and health care practitioners. Any good bookshop is likely to have a significantly sized self-help section.

Self-help books are often amongst the top ten best-selling books. In America and Great Britain, a number of self-help materials have been assessed and been shown to be effective. Recent research has shown that self-help materials can be a helpful way of teaching life skills and of tackling problems such as distress, anxiety and depression.

Learning about Post-Traumatic Stress Disorder

In our everyday lives, any of us can have an experience that is overwhelming, frightening and beyond our control. Most people, in time, get over experiences like this without needing help. In some people though, traumatic experiences set off a reaction that can last for many months or years. This is called Post-Traumatic Stress Disorder, or PTSD for short.

People who have repeatedly experienced:

- ❑ severe neglect or abuse as an adult or as a child;

- ❑ severe repeated violence of abuse as an adult, e.g., torture, abusive imprisonment

can have a similar set of reactions. This is called 'complex PTSD' and is described later in this chapter.

How does PTSD start?

Post-Traumatic Stress Disorder can start after any traumatic event. A traumatic event is one where we can see that we are in danger, our life is threatened, or where we see other people dying or being injured. Some typical traumatic events would be: violent personal assault (sexual assault, rape, physical attack, abuse, robbery, mugging). Even hearing about the unexpected injury or violent death of a family member or close friend can start PTSD.

When does PTSD start?

The symptoms of PTSD can start after a delay of weeks, or even months. They usually appear within six months of a traumatic event.

What does PTSD feel like?

Many people feel grief-stricken, depressed, anxious, guilty and angry after a traumatic experience. As well as these understandable emotional reactions, there are three main types of symptoms produced by such an experience:

1. Flashbacks and nightmares

You find yourself re-living the event, again and again. This can happen both as a 'flashback' in the day, and as nightmares when you are asleep. These can be so realistic that it feels as though you are living through the experience all over again. You see it in your mind, but may also feel the emotions and physical sensations of what happened – fear, sweating, smells, sounds, pain.

Ordinary things can trigger off flashbacks. For instance, if you had a car crash in the rain, a rainy day might start a flashback.

2. Avoidance and numbing

It can be just too upsetting to re-live your experience over and over again. So you distract yourself. You keep your mind busy by losing yourself in a hobby, working very hard, or spending your time absorbed in a crossword or jigsaw puzzles. You avoid places and people that remind you of the trauma, and try not to talk about it.

You may deal with the pain of your feelings by trying to feel nothing at all – by becoming emotionally numb. You communicate less with other people, who then find it hard to live or work with you.

3. Being 'on guard'

You find that you stay alert all the time, as if you are looking out for danger. You can't relax. This is called 'hypervigilance'. You feel anxious and find it hard to sleep. Other people will notice that you are jumpy and irritable.

Other symptoms

Emotional reactions to stress are often accompanied by:

- ❑ muscle aches and pains
- ❑ diarrhoea
- ❑ irregular heartbeats

- ❑ headaches
- ❑ feelings of panic and fear
- ❑ depression
- ❑ drinking too much alcohol
- ❑ using drugs (including painkillers).

Why are traumatic events so shocking?

They undermine our sense that life is fair, reasonably safe, and that we are secure. A traumatic experience makes it very clear that we can die at any time. The symptoms of PTSD are part of a normal reaction to narrowly avoided death.

Does everyone get PTSD after a traumatic experience?

No. But nearly everyone will have the symptoms of post-traumatic stress for the first month or so. This is because they help to keep you going, and help you to understand the experience you have been through. This is an 'acute stress reaction'. Over a few weeks, most people slowly come to terms with what has happened, and their stress symptoms start to disappear.

Not everyone is so lucky. About one in three people will find that their symptoms just carry on and that they can't come to terms with what has happened. It is as though the process has got stuck. The symptoms of post-traumatic stress, although normal in themselves, become a problem – or PTSD – when they go on for too long.

What makes PTSD worse?

The more disturbing the experience, the more likely you are to develop PTSD. The most traumatic events:

- ❑ are sudden and unexpected
- ❑ go on for a long time
- ❑ you are trapped and can't get away
- ❑ involve children.

If you are in a situation where you continue to be exposed to stress and uncertainty, this will make it difficult or impossible for your PTSD symptoms to improve.

What about ordinary 'stress'?

Everybody feels stressed from time to time. Unfortunately, the word 'stress' is used to mean two rather different things:

- ❑ our inner sense of worry, feeling tense or feeling burdened;

or

- ❑ the problems in our life that are giving us these feelings. This could be work, relationships, maybe just trying to get by without much money.

Unlike PTSD, these things are with us, day in and day out. They are part of normal, everyday life, but can produce anxiety, depression, tiredness and headaches. They can also make some physical problems worse, such as stomach ulcers and skin problems. These are certainly troublesome, but they are not the same as PTSD.

Why does PTSD happen?

We don't know for certain. There are a several possible explanations for why PTSD occurs.

Psychological

When we are frightened, we remember things very clearly. Although it can be distressing to remember these things, it can help us to understand what happened and, in the long run, help us to survive.

❑ The flashbacks, or replays, force us to think about what has happened. We can decide what to do if it happens again. After a while, we learn to think about it without becoming upset.

❑ It is tiring and distressing to remember a trauma. Avoidance and numbing keep the number of replays down to a manageable level.

❑ Being 'on guard' means that we can react quickly if another crisis happens.

❑ But we don't want to spend the rest of our life going over it. We only want to think about it when we have to – if we find ourselves in a similar situation.

How do I know when I've got over a traumatic experience?

When you can:

❑ think about it without becoming distressed

❑ not feel constantly under threat

❑ not think about it at inappropriate times.

Why is PTSD often not recognised?

❑ None of us like to talk about upsetting events and feelings.

❑ We may not want to admit to having symptoms, because we don't want to be thought of as weak or mentally unstable.

❑ Doctors and other professionals are human too. They may feel uncomfortable if we try to talk about gruesome or horrifying events.

❑ People with PTSD often find it easier to talk about the other problems that go along with it – headache, sleep problems, irritability, depression, tension, substance abuse, family or work-related problems.

How can I tell if I have PTSD?

Have you have experienced a traumatic event of the sort described here? If you have, do you:

- ❏ have vivid memories, flashbacks or nightmares?
- ❏ avoid things that remind you of the event?
- ❏ feel emotionally numb at times?
- ❏ feel irritable and constantly on edge but can't see why?
- ❏ eat more than usual, or use more drink or drugs than usual?
- ❏ feel out of control of your mood?
- ❏ find it more difficult to get on with other people?
- ❏ have to keep very busy to cope?
- ❏ feel depressed or exhausted?

If it is less than six weeks since the traumatic event, and these experiences are slowly improving, they may be part of the normal process of adjustment.

If it is more than six weeks since the event, and these experiences don't seem to be getting better, it is worth talking it over with your doctor.

How can PTSD be helped?

Helping yourself

Do ...

- ❏ keep life as normal as possible
- ❏ get back to your usual routine
- ❏ talk about what happened to someone you trust
- ❏ try relaxation exercises
- ❏ go back to work
- ❏ eat and exercise regularly
- ❏ go back to where the traumatic event happened
- ❏ take time to be with family and friends
- ❏ drive with care – your concentration may be poor
- ❏ be more careful generally – accidents are more likely at this time
- ❏ speak to a doctor

❑   expect to get better.

Don't ...

❑   beat yourself up about it – PTSD symptoms are not a sign of weakness. They are a normal reaction, of normal people, to terrifying experiences

❑   bottle up your feelings. If you have developed PTSD symptoms, don't keep it to yourself because treatment is usually very successful

❑   avoid talking about it

❑   expect the memories to go away immediately, they may be with you for quite some time

❑   expect too much of yourself. Cut yourself a bit of slack while you adjust to what has happened

❑   stay away from other people

❑   drink lots of alcohol or coffee or smoke more

❑   get overtired

❑   miss meals

❑   take holidays on your own.

What can interfere with getting better?

You may find that other people will:

❑   not let you talk about it

❑   avoid you

❑   be angry with you

❑   think of you as weak

❑   blame you.

These are all ways in which other people protect themselves from thinking about gruesome or horrifying events. It won't help you because it doesn't give you the chance to talk over what has happened to you.

You may not be able to talk easily about it. A traumatic event can put you into a trance-like state which makes the situation seem unreal or bewildering. It is harder to deal with if you can't remember what happened, can't put it into words, or can't make sense of it.

Treatment

Just as there are both physical and psychological aspects to PTSD, so there are both physical and psychological treatments for it.

Psychotherapy

All the effective psychotherapies for PTSD focus on the traumatic experiences that have produced your symptoms rather than your past life. You cannot change or forget what has happened. You can learn to think differently about it, about the world, and about your life.

You need to be able to remember what happened, as fully as possible, without being overwhelmed by fear and distress. These therapies help you to put words to the traumatic experiences that you have had. By remembering the event, going over it and making sense of it, your mind can do its normal job, of storing the memories away and moving on to other things.

If you can start to feel safe again and in control of your feelings, you won't need to avoid the memories as much. Indeed, you can gain more control over your memories so that you only think about them when you want to, rather than having them erupt into your mind spontaneously.

These treatments should all be given by specialists in the treatment of PTSD. The sessions should be at least weekly, with the same therapist and should usually continue for 8–12 weeks. Although sessions will usually last around an hour, they may sometimes last up to 90 minutes.

Cognitive Behavioural Therapy (CBT) is a way of helping you to think differently about your memories, so that they become less distressing and more manageable. It will usually also involve some relaxation work to help you tolerate the discomfort of thinking about the traumatic events.

EMDR (Eye Movement Desensitisation & Reprocessing) is a technique which uses eye movements to help the brain to process flashbacks and to make sense of the traumatic experience. It may sound odd, but it has been shown to work.

Group therapy involves meeting with a group of other people who have been through the same, or a similar traumatic event. The fact that other people in the group have some idea of what you have been through can make it much easier to talk about what has happened.

Medication

SSRI antidepressant tablets will both reduce the strength of PTSD symptoms and relieve any depression that is also present. They will need to be prescribed by a doctor.

This type of medication should not make you sleepy, although they all have some side effects in some people. They may also produce unpleasant symptoms if stopped quickly, so the dose should usually be reduced gradually. If they are helpful, you should carry on taking them for around 12 months. Soon after starting an antidepressant, some people may find that they feel more:

- ❑ anxious

- ❑ restless

- ❑ suicidal.

Occasionally, if someone is so distressed that they cannot sleep or think clearly, anxiety-reducing medication may be necessary. These tablets should usually not be prescribed for more than 10 days or so.

Body-focused therapies

These can help to control the distress of PTSD. They can also reduce hyperarousal, or the feeling of being 'on guard' all the time. These therapies include physiotherapy and osteopathy, but also complementary therapies such as massage, acupuncture, reflexology, yoga, meditation and tai chi. They all help you to develop ways of relaxing and managing stress.

Effectiveness of treatments

At present, there is evidence that EMDR, CBT and antidepressants are all effective. There is not enough information for us to say that one of these treatments is better than another. There is no evidence that other forms of psychotherapy or counselling are helpful to PTSD.

Complex PTSD

This can start weeks or months after the traumatic event, but may take years to be recognised for what they are. As well as the symptoms of PTSD described above, you may:

- ❑ feel shame and guilt

- ❑ have a sense of numbness, a lack of feelings in your body

- ❑ be unable to enjoy anything

- ❑ control your emotions by using street drugs, alcohol, or by harming yourself

- ❑ cut yourself off from what is going on around you (dissociation)

- ❑ have physical symptoms caused by your distress

- ❑ find that you can't put your emotions into words

- ❑ want to kill yourself

- ❑ take risks and do things on the 'spur of the moment'.

What makes PTSD worse?

If:

- ❑ it happens at an early stage – the earlier the age, the worse the trauma

- ❑ it is caused by a parent or other care giver

- ❏ the trauma is severe
- ❏ the trauma goes on for a long time
- ❏ you are isolated
- ❏ you are still in touch with the abuser and/or threats to your safety.

How does it come about?

The earlier the trauma happens, the more it affects psychological development. Some children cope by being defensive or aggressive, while others cut themselves off from what is going on around them. They tend to grow up with a sense of shame and guilt rather than feeling confident and good about themselves.

Getting better

Try to start doing the normal things of life that have nothing to do with your past experiences of trauma. This could include finding friends, getting a job, doing regular exercise, learning relaxation techniques, developing a hobby or having pets. This helps you slowly to trust the world around you.

Lack of trust in other people – and the world in general – is central to complex PTSD. Treatment often needs to be longer to allow you to develop a secure relationship with a therapist – if you like, to experience that it is possible to trust someone in this world without being abused. The work will often happen in three stages:

Stabilisation

You learn how to understand and control your distress and emotional cutting off, or 'dissociation'. This can involve 'grounding' techniques to help you stay in the present – concentrating on ordinary physical feelings that remind you that you are not still living in the traumatic past.

You may also be able to 'disconnect' your physical symptoms of fear and anxiety from the memories and emotions that produce them, making them less frightening.

You start to be able to tolerate day-to-day life without experiencing anxiety and flashbacks. This may sometimes be the only help that is needed.

Trauma-focused therapy

EMDR or CBT (see above) can help you remember your traumatic experiences with less distress and more control. Other psychotherapies, including psychodynamic psychotherapy, can also be helpful. Care needs to be taken in complex PTSD because these treatments can make the situation worse if not used properly.

Reintegration

You begin to develop a new life for yourself. You become able to use your skills or learn new ones and to make satisfying relationships in the real world.

Medication can be used if you feel too distressed or unsafe, or if psychotherapy is not possible. It can include both antidepressants and antipsychotic medication – but not usually tranquillisers or sleeping tablets.

What is CBT?

It is a way of talking about:

- ❑ how you think about yourself, the world and other people; and

- ❑ how what you do affects your thoughts and feelings.

Cognitive Behavioural Therapy can help you to change how you think (Cognitive) and what you do (Behaviour). These changes can help you to feel better. Unlike some of the other talking treatments, it focuses on the 'here and now' problems and difficulties. Instead of focusing on the causes of your distress or symptoms in the past, it looks for ways to improve your state of mind now.

It has been found to be helpful in anxiety, depression, panic, agoraphobia and other phobias, social phobia, bulimia, obsessive compulsive disorder, PTSD and Schizophrenia.

How does it work?
Cognitive Behavioural Therapy can help you to make sense of overwhelming problems by breaking them down into smaller parts. This makes it easier to see how they are connected and how they affect you. These parts are:

- ❑ A situation – a problem, event or difficult situation.

From this can follow:

- ❑ thoughts

- ❑ emotions

- ❑ physical feelings

- ❑ actions.

Situation:	You've had a bad day, feel fed up, so go out shopping. As you walk down the road, someone you know walks by and, apparently, ignores you.	
	Unhelpful	Helpful
Thoughts:	He/she ignored me – they don't like me	He/she looks a bit wrapped up in themselves – I wonder if there's something wrong?

Emotions:	Low, sad and rejected	Concerned for the other person
Physical feelings:	Stomach cramps, low energy, feel sick	None – feel comfortable
Action:	Go home and avoid them	Get in touch to make sure they are OK

The same situation has led to two very different results, depending on how you thought about the situation. How you **think** has affected how you **felt** and what you **did**. In the example, in the left-hand column, you've jumped to a conclusion without very much evidence for it – and this matters because it has led to:

❑ a number of uncomfortable feelings

❑ an unhelpful behaviour.

If you go home feeling depressed, you'll probably brood about what has happened and feel worse. If you get in touch with the other person, there's a good chance you'll feel better about yourself. If you don't, you won't have the chance to correct any misunderstandings about what they think of you – and you will probably feel worse. This is a simplified way of looking at what happens. The whole sequence, and parts of it, can also feedback like this:

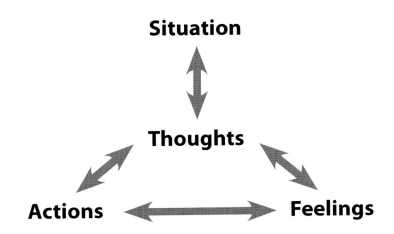

This vicious circle can make you feel worse. It can even create new situations that make you feel worse. You can start to believe quite unrealistic (and unpleasant) things about yourself. This happens because, when we are distressed, we are more likely to jump to conclusions and to interpret things in extreme and unhelpful ways.

Cognitive Behavioural Therapy can help you to break this vicious circle of altered thinking, feelings and behaviour. When you see the parts of the sequence clearly, you can change them – and so change the way you feel. Cognitive Behavioural Therapy aims to get you to a point where you can do it yourself, and work out your own ways of tackling these problems.

'Five areas' assessment

This is another way of connecting all the five areas mentioned above. It builds in our relationships with other people and helps us to see how these can make us feel better or worse. Other issues such as debt, job and housing difficulties are also important. If you improve one area, you are likely to improve other parts of your life as well.

What does CBT involve?

The sessions

Cognitive Behavioural Therapy can be done individually or with a group of people. It can also be done from a self-help book or computer programme. In England and Wales, two computer-based programmes have been approved for use by the NHS. 'Fear Fighter' is for people with phobias or panic attacks, 'Beating the Blues' is for people with mild to moderate depression.

If you have individual therapy:

❑ You will usually meet with a therapist for between 5 and 20, weekly, or fortnightly, sessions. Each session will last between 30 and 60 minutes.

❑ In the first 2–4 sessions, the therapist will check that you can use this sort of treatment and you will check that you feel comfortable with it.

❑ The therapist will also ask you questions about your past life and background. Although CBT concentrates on the here and now, at times you may need to talk about the past to understand how it is affecting you now.

You decide what you want to deal with in the short, medium and long term.

❑ You and the therapist will usually start by agreeing on what to discuss that day.

The work

❑ With the therapist, you break each problem down into its separate parts, as in the example above. To help this process, your therapist may ask you to keep a diary. This will help you to identify your individual patterns of thoughts, emotions, bodily feelings and actions.

❑ Together you will look at your thoughts, feelings and behaviours to work out:
   ❑ if they are unrealistic or unhelpful
   ❑ how they affect each other, and you.

❑ The therapist will then help you to work out how to change unhelpful thoughts and behaviours.

❑ It's easy to talk about doing something, much harder is to actually do it. So, after you have identified what you can change, your therapist will recommend 'homework' – you practise these changes in your everyday life. Depending on the situation, you might start to:

❏ question a self-critical or upsetting thought and replace it with a positive (and more realistic) one that you have developed in CBT;

❏ recognise that you are about to do something that will make you feel worse and, instead, do something more helpful.

❏ At each meeting you discuss how you've got on since the last session. Your therapist can help with suggestions if any of the tasks seem too hard or don't seem to be helping.

❏ They will not ask you to do things you don't want to do – you decide the pace of the treatment and what you will and won't try. The strength of CBT is that you can continue to practise and develop your skills even after the sessions have finished. This makes it less likely that your symptoms or problems will return.

How effective is CBT?

❏ It is one of the most effective treatments for conditions where anxiety or depression is the main problem.

❏ It is the most effective psychological treatment for moderate and severe depression.

❏ It is as effective as antidepressants for many types of depression.

What other treatments are there and how do they compare?

❏ CBT is used in many conditions, so it isn't possible to list them all here. We will look at alternatives to the most common problems – anxiety and depression.

❏ CBT isn't for everyone and another type of talking treatment may work better for you.

❏ CBT is as effective as antidepressants for many forms of depression. It may be slightly more effective than antidepressants in treating anxiety.

❏ For severe depression, CBT should be used with antidepressant medication. When you are very low you may find it hard to change the way you think until antidepressants have started to make you feel better.

❏ Tranquillisers should not be used as a long-term treatment for anxiety. CBT is a better option.

Problems with CBT

❏ If you are feeling low and are having difficulty concentrating, it can be hard, at first, to get the hang of CBT – or, indeed, any psychotherapy.

❏ This may make you feel disappointed or overwhelmed. A good therapist will pace your sessions so you can cope with the work you are trying to do.

❏ It can sometimes be difficult to talk about feelings of depression, anxiety, shame or anger.

How long will the treatment last?

A course may be from six weeks to six months. It will depend on the type of problem and how it is working for you. The availability of CBT varies between different areas and there may be a waiting list for treatment.

What if the symptoms come back?

There is always a risk that the anxiety or depression will return. If they do, your CBT skills should make it easier for you to control them. So, it is important to keep practising your CBT skills, even after you are feeling better. There is some research that suggests CBT may be better than antidepressants at preventing depression coming back. If necessary, you can have a 'refresher' course.

So what impact would CBT have on my life?

Depression and anxiety are unpleasant. They can seriously affect your ability to work and enjoy life. CBT can help you to control the symptoms. It is unlikely to have a negative effect on your life, apart from the time you need to give up to do it.

Psychotherapy

There are many different types of psychotherapy. They are all ways of helping people to overcome stress, emotional problems, relationship problems or troublesome habits. What they have in common is that they are all treatments based on talking to another person and sometimes doing things together. They are the 'talking treatments'. The person carrying out the treatment is usually called a therapist, the person being seen is usually referred to as the client.

Psychodynamic psychotherapy

This focuses on the feelings we have about other people, especially our family and those we are close to. Treatment involves discussing past experiences and how these may have led to our present situation and also how these past experiences may be affecting our life now. The understanding gained frees the person to make choices about what happens in the future.

Psychodynamic psychotherapy may involve quite brief therapy for specific difficulties. If your problems are longstanding, treatment may mean attending regular sessions over many months.

Behavioural psychotherapy

This tries to change patterns of behaviour more directly. Patients can be helped to overcome fears by spending more and more time in the situation they fear, or by learning ways of reducing their anxiety. They may be given 'homework' exercises, and asked to keep diaries or to practise new skills between sessions.
Behavioural psychotherapy is particularly effective for anxiety, panic, phobias, obsessive-compulsive problems and various kinds of social or sexual difficulty. Relief from symptoms often occurs quite quickly.

Can these different approaches work together?

These are very different sorts of treatment, but they all help us to understand better how we work, which can help us to make changes in our lives.
Psychotherapists may use a combination of techniques to suit the individual, and people may progress from, say, individual to group therapy, or marital work to individual treatment.

What actually happens?

Psychotherapy usually involves regular meetings at the same time, same place every week or two weeks. In most cases the length of the treatment will be agreed between the client(s) and the therapist(s) within a month or so of starting. What happens during a session is usually considered confidential to the people in that session.

In individual psychotherapy, one patient and one therapist talk together in a quiet room, usually for 50 minutes or so.

In group therapy, several people with similar sorts of problems meet regularly with a therapist or therapists. These sessions may be longer than in individual psychotherapy. Group therapy may appear less intimate, but it is not a cheap or second-rate treatment – in fact it is the best treatment for some problems. The experience of discovering one is not alone, and of being able to help other people, is powerfully encouraging and is often the first step towards getting better.

Trauma risk management

Previous reactive single session models of post-incident interventions, such as Critical Incident Stress Debriefing, or CISD, have been subjected to scientific scrutiny and shown to not just lack effectiveness, but also have the potential to do harm.

The National Institute for Clinical Excellence (NICE), the UK body which sanctions medical interventions, has issued guidance on the management of post-traumatic illnesses. At the core of the guidelines is the principle of 'not making a meal' of normal levels of post-incident distress. For most individuals, distress is not a medical problem and does not need complex interventions. NICE suggests that for the first month after an incident, a policy of watchful waiting should be employed, with individuals who have been exposed to the event. This does not just mean those who were 'there' but also those who might feel responsible; those who might have been on a radio line or those who had to help with the aftermath.

TRiM is a 'NICE-compliant' model of peer group traumatic stress management which aims to foster high levels of organisational resilience. Although TRiM began within the Royal Marines Commandos, British Elite Amphibious Troops, many other non-military organisations now use TRiM including the Foreign and Commonwealth Office; media organisations including the BBC and the emergency services including the London Ambulance Service and numerous UK police forces. The TRiM model bases itself on keeping employees functioning after traumatic events, by providing support and education to those who require it. Additionally, TRiM aims to identify those who are not coping after potentially traumatising events and it is designed to ensure that they are signposted to professional sources of help. In essence, TRiM aims to empower organisations to discharge their duty of care whilst promoting a proactive and resilient stance to the psychological effects of potentially traumatic events.

TRiM practitioners are non-medical personnel who have received between two and five days of training, enabling them to identify psychological risk factors that might otherwise go unnoticed. The training covers the basics of trauma psychology, how to plan for traumatic events, both before and immediately afterwards and how to conduct a psychological risk assessment. Practitioners are encouraged to use already existing personnel management systems to assist normally distressed individuals in their recovery and, where necessary, ensure that those who require it are referred for appropriate treatment at an early stage.

Counselling

Counselling takes place when a counsellor sees a client in a private and confidential setting to explore a difficulty the client is having, distress they may be experiencing or perhaps their dissatisfaction with life, or loss of a sense of direction and purpose. It is always at the request of the client as no one can properly be 'sent' for counselling. By listening attentively and patiently, the counsellor can begin to perceive the difficulties from the client's point of view and can help them to see things more clearly, possibly from a different perspective. Counselling is a way of enabling choice or change or of reducing confusion. It does not involve giving advice or directing a client to take a particular course of action. Counsellors do not judge or exploit their clients in any way.

In the counselling sessions, the client can explore various aspects of their life and feelings, talking about them freely and openly in a way that is rarely possible with friends or family. Bottled-up feelings such as anger, anxiety, grief and embarrassment can become very intense, and counselling offers an opportunity to explore them, with the possibility of making them easier to understand. The counsellor will encourage the expression of feelings and as a result of their training will be able to accept and reflect the client's problems without becoming burdened by them.

Acceptance and respect for the client are essentials for a counsellor and, as the relationship develops, so too does trust between the counsellor and client, enabling the client to look at many aspects of their life, their relationships and themselves which they may not have considered or been able to face before. The counsellor may help the client to examine in detail the behaviour or situations which are proving troublesome and to find an area where it would be possible to initiate some change as a start. The counsellor may help the client to look at the options open to them and help them to decide the best for them.

CHAPTER SUMMARY

❑ Take advantage of all support that is available.

❑ Take an active role in your recovery, learn about ways in which you can support yourself.

6

WORK MORALE AND ITS LINK WITH ORGANISATIONAL STRESS

The Management Standards and Stress Reduction

The formulation of the stress reduction management standards are a result of research conducted by the Health and Safety Executive in the United Kingdom. Having considered these standards, it is important that every employee understands these working considerations. These standards are not the sole function of management as everybody within the workplace can contribute. It's about developing a stress-reducing culture that is supportive and friendly. It's not someone else's responsibility, but a collective attitude. Every member of staff can contribute or consider these standards every day. This rationale can be incorporated into every briefing, team meeting or policing event. Morale is the 'confidence and enthusiasm of a particular group of people'. These standards when not adhered to, not only place people in a position of stress, they also consistently damage morale and reduce team performance.

One's happiness might seem like a personal subject, but an American researcher says employers should be concerned about the well-being of their employees because it could be the underlying factor to success. Thomas Wright found that when employees have high levels of psychological well-being and job satisfaction, they perform better and are less likely to leave their job –making happiness a valuable tool for maximising organisational outcomes.

'Happiness' is a broad and subjective word, but a person's well-being includes the presence of positive emotions, like joy and interest, and the absence of negative emotions, like apathy and sadness.

An excessive negative focus in the workplace could be harmful, such as performance evaluations where negatives like what an employee failed to do are the focus of concentration. When properly implemented in the workplace environment, positive emotions can enhance employee perceptions of finding meaning in their work. The standards improve workplace happiness and promote harmony.

Demand, support, control, communication, relationships, role and change

The amount of staff that are available at peak demand on any given day has a relationship with each standard. This relationship can be a positive or negative one. I don't wish to dwell on police numbers, but as you will see in the next section, it has an overriding effect on each management standard. With an increased public demand that isn't spread across all departments, the people meeting the demands can become disgruntled. Whilst demand increases, interdepartmental control also increases, this translates into defensiveness. Whilst defensiveness manifests, communication becomes 'blaming' and counterproductive. The role of individual officers and their intimate boundaries become invaded and a struggle ensues. They begin to think, "Why am I dealing with this issue? Surely this is for x, y and z department?" Relationships deteriorate and infighting develops. This cycle repeats itself and management realise that something must be 'wrong'. Change is brought about and this isn't communicated correctly, which in turn frustrates officers once more. The cycle moves on and on. An experienced police officer that I have had the fortune of working with said, "Divide and conquer". By ignoring demand, control, communication, relationships, role and change, the mindset of the frontline becomes divisive and morale is 'conquered'.

Within these identified standards, there are a number of strands that cross over the entire process and they include training, communication and technology.

Communication

A wise person once said, "You have two ears and one mouth, communicate within those proportions". The police service traditionally uses a structured month-by-month system to discuss interdepartmental issues such as resources, performance, planning, intelligence, health and safety, etc. Usually, supervisors and the senior management meet and then decide upon courses of action for particular issues. These meetings are usually private and are held behind closed doors. There is usually an element of secrecy. Prior to the meetings, there is very little consultation with frontline staff. The topics of each meeting are not published and disseminated to the frontline. Prior to the meetings, there are usually discussions about who and what is going to happen. A great deal of speculation and worry exists among frontline staff. Questions like "Will I be moved? Will my shifts change?" When the inevitable happens, rumours begin to start and this can impact on morale. When officers are not consulted about a shift change or an internal move and are then told it was discussed in the resource management meeting, there is a feeling of being let down by the management team. Police officers can be moved to any part of the force area, for no particular reason, but this doesn't excuse the organisation. There still needs to be consultation and communication. Closed door management meetings undermine 'control, communication, relationships and change'.

Training

The type of training that I am talking about doesn't have to be structured and results-driven. Within your organisation, there exists people who are experts in their various fields. You may not think of them as experts, but their combined knowledge could save you a great amount of time and effort. A simple 20-minute presentation could be enough to explain a new method of working. Traditionally, all training is compiled by the local training officer (all the mandatory training). There is nothing more effective than a presentation delivered by your peers. You could invite various people to give a talk about their area of expertise. Presentations could encompass real operational scenarios.

Technology

The use of handheld data, ANPR, head-mounted cameras, laptops, digital cameras, e-learning, internet solutions and real-time briefing has had a defining effect within the police service. Our operational methods of communication are far more effective, intelligence can be delivered within an instant and the means for operational safety have improved. Updating incidents, victims and management actions can all be completed whilst out in the field. This is a positive from the perspective of the management standards. Technology alone doesn't solve our human problems altogether, fear and aversion are human factors and need a human response.

Demands

Includes issues like workload, work patterns and the work environment

The standard is that:

- ❑ employees indicate that they are able to cope with the demands of their jobs;

- ❑ the organisation provides employees with adequate and achievable demands in relation to the agreed hours of work;

- ❑ people's skills and abilities are matched to the job demands;

- ❑ employees' concerns about their work environment are addressed.

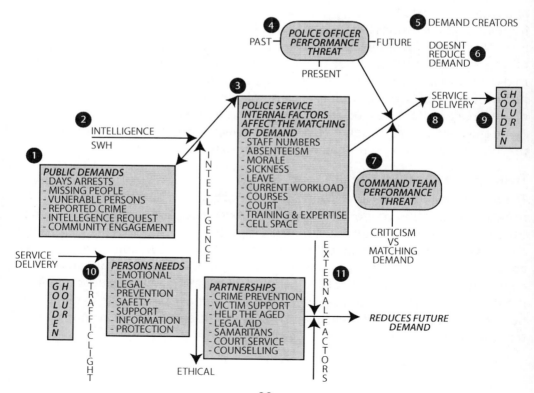

Demand ①

Demand comprises of the day's arrests, missing people, reported crime, intelligence requirement, ongoing incidents and community engagement.

Demand has a two-way relationship with a number of factors. The demands of the day interconnect with the amount of suitably qualified staff that can match daily demands. The right amount of people, who are suitably trained, suitably motivated and in possession of the latest intelligence are the people who can reduce demand.

Whilst we observe daily demand, we can make the simile of that of a doctor observing a patient's disease. I think that the word 'dis-ease' is a perfect description of the people who create a policing demand. They are not at ease and a certain amount of chaos surrounds them. Chaos translates into the person's manifestation of a particular crime. The doctor needs medical testing and diagnosis in order to diagnose what the problem is. The doctor uses a variety of instruments and procedures to gain the correct amount of information. In this sense, the doctor's measurement is our 'policing intelligence' and intelligence is based in six questions. Who? What? Why? Where? When? How? Without intelligence we are not effectively gathering the correct information that can support the control and intervention of societies dis-ease. The definition of stress comes very close to an adapted definition of demand.

Stress:

'A particular relationship between the person and the environment that is appraised by the person as taxing and exceeding his or her resources and endangering his or her well-being.'

Demand:

'A particular relationship between the organisation and the public environment that is appraised by the organisation as taxing resources.'

Policing involves observing, responding, controlling and preventing. Simply, policing demands can be reduced by a number of distinct phases of policing activity. On a daily basis, in terms of our reported crime, what crimes or activities are creating the greatest amount of demand? What intelligence do we have about these types of crimes? Who? What? Why? Where? When? How? ②

What resources can we deploy to access this intelligence? What information can our internal and external partnerships and communities give us? Do we have sufficient policing resources to act on this intelligence?

When are we going to act on this information? Many studies have shown that targeted intelligence and proactive arrests actually decrease demand. Crime is usually committed by a handful of individuals. So, it sounds simple, almost too easy, what gets in the way?

Internal factors ③

Staff numbers, absenteeism, sickness, annual leave, training courses, court appearances, morale and motivation, current workload all play a part in reducing the response to daily demand.

The culture of performance, a threat to reducing demand ④

The service promotes performance and it is the key to being a good all-round performing police officer. In the locker room, this issue is discussed at length with new and experienced police officers. The inexperienced police officer will arrest anyone for any offence as long as they can 'tick the box' and offer fresh evidence of his/her skills and abilities. The experienced officer is hesitant and considers all the other options. If the policing culture creates a demand for arrests, summons, intelligence and minor processes, a number of obvious practices begin to surface.

At the PC level, easy arrests and minor processes become the officer's daily goal. Examples include fail to appear warrants, drink driving, public order arrests (when they could have gone home), disqualified driving and simple possession of drugs. These types of offences are easy and only require a written statement and a small file of evidence.

At the shift level, other officers begin to see the officer's pro-activity and begin to model such behaviours. The shift begins to steer in the direction of easy, achievable targets. The supervisor recognises his/her shift achievements and congratulates them. The management team also recognise such blatant pro-activity, resounding success follows.

The individual officer, although working hard, may not be attending to the current daily intelligence picture. There has been a daily spike in reported dwelling burglaries; however, the 'good' officer has submitted reams of paperwork that doesn't relate to the here and now. This is problematic in many senses, who is actually analysing the crime needs and patterns when the 'good officer' is busy with a drink driving arrest? The next day, a number of dwelling burglaries are reported once again and the cycle repeats itself across each shift and department. Demand begins to rise steadily.

Past, present and future demand

Picture the scene, six police officers are being briefed with regard to the morning's activities. The supervisor asks each officer what they have planned for today.

PC John says: "I have three statements to take from a robbery that happened two weeks ago and one outstanding suspect to arrest."

PC Williams says: "I have last night's arrest to deal with."

PC Ball says: "I want to go out and arrest as many people on warrant as I can."

PC John's work is in the past, PC Williams' work involves the present and PC Ball's working ethos involves creating demand. The hours tick past and even more work is created, the day's demand is becoming greater. The day unfolds and, remember, we have very little control of how the day will unfold. As a team of police officers doing the best we can in trying circumstances, surely it would make more sense to split the team into a team of individuals who work together to catch up with past enquiries and to deal with the demands of the day? By doing this as a team, we are effectively reducing the team's demand. After demand is managed, then we can effectively plan to create demand more if need be. This ensures that the demands of the organisation become adequate and achievable on a day-to-day and moment-by-moment basis. Focus on the demand of here and now and sweep up past demand as a team. This shift will ensure that each officer can cope with daily demand.

Beware the demand creators 5

The culture of easy performance creates a hole in the actual world of demand. Who is actually dealing with all the work? If a team is focusing solely on the quick arrests hits, then who is doing the more protracted and difficult work? Officers who engage in creating demand are actually placing greater demands on their fellow officers and fellow teams. Limit those officers who are creating unnecessary demand.

Workload and demand 6

Thoughtless delegation is the key to poor workload allocation. PC Jones says: "A sergeant I worked with some years ago was an excellent delegator. Every task was shared out, every officer had three tasks per day. All equal and fair. After a month of this process, I met him in the office and asked if we could have a talk. I said, 'I won't be able to go out next week, I have five people to arrest and I have to take 15 statements. I will also have to submit five files of evidence.' After explaining that I had all this work to do, he looked at me with exasperation. It hadn't dawned on him to assess the needs of each task and prioritise accordingly."

Golden hour 9

Identify within your place of work the activities that come back and require more attention and detail. These activities are telling you something, you must invest more time and effort at the very start of these activities. The 'golden hour' is a term used by investigators that seeks to improve the quality of an investigation. The first few moments of a crime being committed are crucial and it is within the first hour that crimes are solved. Energy and focus within the 'golden hour' will save countless hours of further statements and enquiries. By seizing the initiative and getting as much detail as possible, you create the very likely conditions that an offender will admit guilt and a guilty plea will be entered at court. This will serve to reduce additional paper work and cut attendance at court proceedings. We all know that the courts don't care about our days off. **The golden hour is what it says it is. Remind yourself that every action has an equal and opposite reaction. If need be, revisit the section on 'Time Management'.**

Criticism vs. matching demand

It's Monday morning and daily tasking is taking place. All the individual departmental heads are busy discussing what needs to be addressed and what incidents need to be developed. In the last ten years there have been dozens of enquiries relating to police procedure, investigation, actions and ethical conduct. An enquiry always changes the police service as we learn the lessons from other force areas and attempt to better ourselves. Enquiries have focused on racism, domestic violence, suicide, murder investigation, missing persons, crowd control and anti-social behaviour. Every aspect of policing has become important as we have learnt the lessons of court cases, media attention and litigation. I believe that this culture of litigation has added to the issues of fear-based policing. How can every aspect of policing activity become important?

I see this on a daily basis as daily tasking sometimes focuses on issues that have been subject to enquiries. The message from the top is filtered down to the frontline 'We need to address this issue, we may get criticised if we don't'. I fully respect the culture and times that we live in, and I understand the rationale behind this type of thinking. This type of thinking is based on our defensive/aversive thinking patterns and it doesn't actually address the present moment and what is actually happening in the here and now. Aversion is based on a reaction and doesn't consider all the factors relating to the actual incident. **7**

Instead of asking the question "Will I be criticised if I don't attend to this incident?" a defensive standpoint, ask the following questions:

Will further physical harm come to this person if I don't act now?

If I don't act now, will this incident create further demand for me and my colleagues? A proactive standpoint.

The first question determines if an incident is URGENT and the second question determines if an incident is IMPORTANT.

Once the incident has been identified as URGENT and IMPORTANT we really need to begin to understand the needs, concerns and expectations of the persons involved in the incident. The police service traditionally has a policy that covers what needs to be done. This sometimes can create even more work, when by actually identifying the persons needs we can match those needs with the appropriate resource and partnership agency. The reason for this increase in work is the forced application of policy that doesn't meet the needs of the person.

Needs	Referrals to
Emotional support	Counselling / Samaritans
Crime prevention advice	Specialist Crime Prevention Officer
Language	Interpreters
Cultural needs	Advice from Specialist Persons
Understanding the legal system	Referral to an online presentation
Police procedure	Detailed explanation

Needs

Ownership

Specialists

Concerns

Communication

Retaliation

Press / Gossip

Expectations

Referrals to

OIC identified

External factors

Demand and staffing levels

Staffing levels are the most talked about issue within the police service. Why is this so? At an early time in our lives we are taught to co-operate, to engage in team work and support one another. Team work is an intrinsic nature of our human experience. To inter-relate and become interdependent on one another is a great achievement. Our working lives become enriched and the organisation's health improves. Health coincidentally means 'whole'. So our health includes the bigger picture, a way of systems thinking. Staffing levels are not in themselves responsible for poor morale. What is responsible and obvious to staff is the mismanagement of resources.

The Police Research Series Paper 143 says:
'Stress caused by insufficient police numbers and increasing workloads was also frequently highlighted as a major cause of absence. Stress will continue to impact on absence levels unless there is a significant increase in staff resources, or more informed deployment practices and better management of shift patterns to ensure appropriate staffing levels and workload equity, which in theory could be achieved without necessarily employing more people.'

We all have probably been involved in team sports at one time in our lives. The anticipation of playing a neighbouring team is exciting, challenging and can sometimes be a little daunting. Prior to the game commencing, the team begins to assemble in the changing rooms.

The most committed team members are always first, ready and prepared. The boots are on and he/she backslaps the incoming team members. One by one, the players arrive. Whispers and phone calls start to be made. The coach says "Have you seen so and so, he's late?" The players start to ring the missing key players. A sense of dread starts to develop. The players start to worry 'we ain't going to win if our captain doesn't show'. In team sports we are vulnerable at those times, we realise that our playing ability depends on others.

The clock is ticking, the temperature is rising, the players start to focus on the opposing team. Are they bigger than us? Are they more motivated than us? Do they have a full team?

It's two minutes before kickoff and we still don't have a full team. The stand-in players are chosen and the team is physically weakened. The players are apprehensive, the psychological mantra begins: 'we are beaten before we start'.

The game begins and it's back between the posts every five minutes. The team gets a thrashing.

The team phenomenon that I have described equally applies to police officers. Parading with two or three response officers, while a town of 25,000 is eating, drinking and getting drunk in the middle of summer. This not just daunting, but frightening and dangerous.

Psychologically these are the most draining times, the stress begins in the parade room whilst sipping a cup of tea. Whilst for some it begins the moment they wake up. The looks that officers give are akin to a novice boxer stepping in the ring with a pro. The evening's work hasn't even started at this point.

The solution I hear is always the same, 'employ more police officers'. This solution I see as a headquarters issue and not something that the local commander can remedy. But the local solution is simple.

1. Get all night staff and partnership agencies to brief and talk together. Response officers, community officers, special constables, firearms officers, dog handlers, street pastors, door supervisors, St John's ambulance and licensees.

2. Offer a comprehensive financial incentive for police officers to recruit locally known and trusted police specials (volunteer officers).

3. Match every serving police officer with a volunteer officer, develop a mentoring scheme and allow the officer a degree of flexibility. Give the individual officer a degree of freedom.

4. Develop an incentives pack and suitable financial reward for volunteer police officers.

5. Crossover shifts from various departments, so in effect, at the peak of demand, there are enough officers to reduce demand.

6. Regular non-uniform police officers and senior officers should spend a proportion of their working week assisting with frontline duties. I explained previously that police officers 'ethically observe'. By placing staff back into core policing each week, it gives a fresh insight into staff 'observation'.

Visible partnership working decreases demand

In terms of team and personality dynamics, spending time on the frontline will allow senior officers to observe the reality of what is going on within the rank and file and not what they are being 'told' by others. This practice will also keep staff members used to wearing a uniform and completing local procedures.

Volunteering can reduce demand

PC James says: "It's Sunday morning and ten people have been arrested the night before. There are only five police officers working and the demands of the night's antics have resulted in a need to take 25 good-quality statements. It takes two hours per statement, realistically only eight will be taken. That means that the file quality and the speed of administering justice will certainly falter. The knock-on effect is seen the following week when the same people are arrested. It's not that difficult to solve, there are countless writing circles, students, writers, ex-police officers and kind-hearted people. Why don't we ask for statement-taking volunteers? Training could be administered in one day and an army of helpers could be on hand to assist the police the next morning." Volunteering is the key to an enhanced service.

Cross training

The greatest winning sporting teams always have someone who can play in different positions. Could cross training members of a department be the answer? Do written statements always need to be conducted by a police officer?

The traffic light system 🔟

Many crime management systems use a traffic light system to highlight and manage demand. Red crimes need immediate attention and amber crimes are a cause for concern. PC Jones had a meeting with his supervisor regarding his apparent poor performance. PC Jones, a well-organised and thoroughly competent officer, was effectively threatened about his apparent failings. His supervisor demanded immediate answers to his failing crime investigations. PC Jones was carrying a heavy workload within the peak of summer. He wasn't alone as other members of the shift were also carrying a high number of crime investigations.

Take, for example, a red light at a set of traffic lights. The light turns red and every car on the road has to stop and observe the colour of the red light. The car behind doesn't hoot its horn and demand why the car in front has stopped. Every car driver accepts that the red light is a signal to stop, observe and think. Similarly, an officer with a heavy workload and a high number of red crimes is indicating that current demands are exceeding the officer's resources. If you're a supervisor reading this paragraph, whatever you do, don't point the finger and blame. This will be perceived as being overbearing and controlling. Stop, observe and think. How can I effectively reduce this team's demand? You will be thanked for your wisdom.

Team dynamics vs. skills and abilities

The Inspector's notice board reveals a great deal about his/her outlook. All the officer's particular skills and training qualifications are written on the team board. I can see how the needs of the organisation outweigh team dynamics and morale. The Inspector may allocate the team a van driver, a PSU officer, a rape-trained officer and a tutor. Great, it all looks good on paper. I've just started my shift with a reluctant van driver, a blame-shifting statement taker and an aversive, hot-tempered community officer. The personality traits that dominate my shift are negative. They could be balanced by a number of individuals who create the opposing environment. Many psychologists have commented on the role of balancing personality traits vs. work allocation. **Focusing on people's skills and abilities and matching them to the job demands should not be the only consideration.**

The summer blues and annual leave

The peak of summer (mid-August) is the yearly time when morale is at its lowest. I don't have any evidence to substantiate this claim, but go to any police station and walk into the parade room. You will see mountains of paper strewn across the room, the bins will be overflowing, empty food cartons will be perched next to computers and officers will be annoyed by the mere sight of you. It's really tense at those times.

Looking at the crime / incidents / anti-social behaviour statistics, crime steadily rises, the temperature and longer daylight hours add to this picture.

PC Baylis explains:

"Unwittingly the police service doesn't plan its resources very well. I can explain the rationale behind my claim. I had a meeting with my sergeant last week, we were discussing annual leave. 'I have decided to book regular time off, with working shifts and dealing with the stresses of police work, I feel that I will be able to recuperate better, could I possibly book off three days a month?'

'The shifts that you have chosen are on weekends and are busy ones, you can't book leave like this,' he said. He added to the conversation, 'You need to book two weeks in the summer, two weeks in the winter and one week in the spring, that's what we do, you know that.'

The hypocrisy in his words was astounding. Here I was trying to book off a weekend in February, and I was getting a flat refusal; however, I knew that the whole shift would be off over August! Exactly at the busiest time! I was doing the job a service, not the other way round.

The consequence of this rigid approach is that during the summer, everyone is competing to take peak summer leave. The shift simply never see one another, when you add into the equation sickness and courses. The frontline is seriously depleted, and depleted during the busiest period. This impacts on performance, morale, sickness etc. **Flexibility is the key to seeing the bigger picture.**

There are many positives of adopting a more flexible and person-centred approach. The officer may have had a weekend of sheer hell, surely it would be better to cast aside a rigid leave allocation to one that serves the emotional needs of each officer? Our emotions and feelings sway at times and at the peak of negative stress, our behaviour can change.

This approach I have only witnessed once. Following a domestic murder, the officers who attended were given two days' leave and the appropriate after care. The Inspector who organised this common-sense approach saw the pitfalls of expecting too much from his officers and realised that significant 'emotional overlap' would hinder morale, performance and absenteeism.

By focusing on the officer's needs, the organisation is saying 'it cares', the exact opposite to what officers will be saying in police stations across the entire globe.

Watch what happens when officers are exposed to too much frontline stress. You may have seen it yourself. The good cop becomes a bad cop. Disciplinary offences, even criminal actions. It is not that the officer isn't professional or standards have fallen, it is a case of too much exposure to stressful conditions leads to decreased performance, attitude and behaviour change.

How does this shift reduce demand?

This proactive standpoint delivers at the police officer, supervisor and command team level. Each rung of policing is working in unison and unnecessary incidents are being bypassed for incidents that are creating more demand and, ultimately, can cause more harm to individuals, families, groups and communities.

Reducing Demand Factors	Police Officer	Supervisor	Senior Officer
Personal Style	Learns to manage demands as opposed to creating demand	Thinks 'shift' demand management as opposed to 'individual' demand management	Indentifies struggling shifts and supervisors and supports
Training	Ensures training courses are relevant to daily demand Officers working in a busy city centre don't necessarily need training in drink drive procedures, rape and violent crime training are more beneficial	Identifies shifts training needs and relevance to operational demands. Considers dual training for some officers	
Absenteeism	Ensures optimal health and actively reduces sickness	Proactively improves morale and working conditions	Proactively improves morale and working conditions
Motivation	Maintains personal motivation through lifestyle factors	Maintains personal motivation through lifestyle factors	
Annual Leave	Spreads leave entitlement across the whole of the year	Ensures adequate staffing across all periods, explains this need to all staff	
Court Appearances	Apply the golden hour thereby maximising evidence and increasing the likelihood of a guilty plea at court	Ensures high-quality file preparation	Ensures resources are at a maximum in order to gather all available evidence
Time Management, Current Workload			

Includes the encouragement, sponsorship and resources provided by the organisation, line management and colleagues

The standard is that:

- ❑ employees indicate that they receive adequate information and support from their colleagues and superiors; and

- ❑ systems are in place locally to respond to any individual concerns.

What should be happening/states to be achieved:

- ❑ the organisation has policies and procedures to adequately support employees;

- ❑ systems are in place to enable and encourage managers to support their staff;

- ❑ systems are in place to enable and encourage employees to support their colleagues;

- ❑ employees know what support is available and how and when to access it;

- ❑ employees know how to access the required resources to do their job; and

- ❑ employees receive regular and constructive feedback.

Our needs change from day to day, as does the daily demands of policing. Integrating support within the context of daily briefings and asking the right questions we can begin to understand the daily needs of ourselves, colleagues and organisation. Our aim is to provide a supporting blanket that can match an individual's needs with the correct amount of support from other sources. The following table illustrates the type of daily support issues that need to be considered. Each supporting consideration is easily achieved.

Supporting Need	Police Officer	Police Supervisor	Senior Officer
Physiological			
Food	Places dried food in personal locker and prepare meals	Plan for refreshment breaks on each shift Organises a 'tuck shop'	Ensures that vending machines and eating facilities are in place
Water	Ensures that water is carried	Plans for refreshment breaks on each shift	Drinking water dispensers to be provided in each working room

Supporting Need	Police Officer	Police Supervisor	Senior Officer
Rest	Asks for quiet time after a difficult incident	Ensures officers are protected from further demands and are given a break	Provides a quiet room or recreational facility (gymnasium or pool room)
Sleep	Prepares for sleep cycles	Gives tired officers an early finish and remind them of the importance of sleep	Plans resources to complement the effects of sleep deprivation
		Drive tired officers home	Drive tired officers home
Fitness	Uses time before or after work for personal fitness	Gives officers time to exercise during duty time	Provides a small station gymnasium for all staff
Financial			
Overtime Expenses Meal claims Other incentives	Understands which expenses can be claimed for	Encourages officers to apply for expenses	Places a notice board in the corridor that answers particular questions about financial entitlements
Emotional			
Access to support services Quiet reflection Befriending Colleague support	Understands which self-help and emotional support services are available	Identifies officers at an early stage that need emotional support	Places a notice board in the corridor that answers particular questions
		Refers officers to support services	Gives each officer a copy of 'Morale matters'
			Reviews incidents and refers officers to support services
	Accesses Stress Assessment	Advises officers to stress assess	Provides stress assessment software

Supporting Need	Police Officer	Police Supervisor	Senior Officer
Safety Health and safety Threat assessment Sickness	Understands 'near misses' and health and safety reporting procedure	Risk assesses current policing practices and walk through the police station and patrol hotspots Report findings	Ensures adequate training is in place
	Double crewed vs. Single crewed / resources vs. demand	Double crewed vs. Single crewed / resources vs. demand	Double crewed vs. Single crewed / resources vs. demand
Social Team dynamics Group support News Groups Events	Ensures each member of your team is involved within team activities Invites new members to participate in sports groups Shares good news with colleagues	Supports extracurricular activities Understands team dynamics Allows officers time to engage in healthy activities Supports a yearly station event	Encourages police sport and police activities Supports a yearly morale boosting event Reduces staff movement to a minimum
Self-esteem Self-confidence Personal development	Identifies areas of improvement via Personal Development Reviews Seeks new opportunities	Identifies opportunities for staff development Utilises training, networking and development opportunities	Allows officers to seek new opportunities for inner growth and development

Supporting Need	Police Officer	Police Supervisor	Senior Officer
Work Environment			
Lighting Design Mood Music Information boards Cleanliness Shift patterns	Informs supervisors about the working environment	Informs supervisors about the working environment Assesses monthly the working environment and considers areas of improvement Removes 'Act Now' posters Adds some humour to the office	Introduces blue lighting Introduces music within police cars Introduces office plants and soothing colour schemes Introduces comfortable office furniture Updates support boards Introduces vending machines
	Plans the year ahead and considers shift patterns that clash with other duties	Introduces flexibility with regard to structured shift patterns	Introduces flexibility with regard to structured shift patterns
Training and Equipment			
Up-to-date equipment Demand-reducing equipment Mandatory training Training needs match officer needs	Reviews police equipment Weekly equipment checks Training needs analysis	Checks officer equipment on a weekly basis Identifies individual and shift training needs	Organises strategic training and case reviews Reviews all equipment: computers, software and hardware Matches training and equipment needs to performance goals
Other			
Religious needs Family needs LGBT	Informs staff members about particular needs	Discusses on a monthly basis the needs and concerns of the officer	Discusses on a monthly basis the needs and concerns of the officer

Supporting Need	Police Officer	Police Supervisor	Senior Officer
Reducing Demoralising Practices	Maintains the team ethos at all times		
Counteracting rumours	Accepts officers strengths and weaknesses		
Communication	Avoids spreading rumours	Avoids spreading rumours	Avoids spreading rumours
	Passes heard rumours to supervisors	Counteracts rumours by placing information on a communications board	Counteract rumours by placing information on a communications board
Performance charting	Make no reference to individual performance	Abolishes performance comparisons	Abolishes performance comparisons and charting of station performance, instead focus on the humane team effort
	Avoids 'should', 'could' and blaming statements	Avoids 'should', 'could' and blaming statements	Avoids 'should', 'could' and blaming statements
	Introduces You Said, We Did Communication styles across all departments	Introduces You Said, We Did Communication styles across all departments	Introduces You Said, We Did Communication styles across all departments

The beat officers perspective

Environment

PC Edmunds explains:

"The physical environment that we work within isn't particularly accommodating. When I look around the police station, I see a number of morale-sapping practices. The latest poster on the wall says 'We must treat victims with respect, listen to their needs and support them throughout'. Mrs Jones came to the police station today to make a statement. I ushered her into a bare-looking room, adjacent to the rear custody door. I sat her down in a collapsible old military chair, she wasn't comfortable. As I introduced the statement process, I was rudely interrupted by one of the recently arrested persons swearing. This lasted for some time. Mrs Jones wasn't comfortable and our statement-taking room isn't the best. I have told numerous bosses about this matter and nothing has happened."

Memory is influenced by the ability to perceive and recall. The ability to gain a good witness statement relies on the officer's ability to build a rapport and for the witness to relax. The witness's relaxed state of mind is of paramount importance. Witness statement-taking rooms should be seriously comfortable for both victim and the statement taker, preferably near to an area where refreshments can be made. Noise needs to be reduced to an absolute minimum. **The public and private environment of our police stations is crucial to our success. If we feel comfortable, we feel supported.**

'Act now' posters – Communication

PC Waters explains:

"The police station is littered with 'act now' posters. They tell very busy, educated and professional officers to do the most mundane activities. For example, remember to wash your hands, remember to arrest people for domestic assaults or you may face disciplinary action. This type of message causes officers to feel annoyed with the organisation; a constant reminder that you are being monitored and compared. Many of the messages are loaded with fear and threat: 'failure to act will result in disciplinary action'. This type of organisational marketing offers no personal approach and increases the actions of aversive officers. It affects morale, we don't like it."

A pattern begins to follow within the police station. Differing departments place differing posters telling people to do the most obvious things. Does this really solve the problem? Is this good communication? What happened to talking to one another? Or is it really an outlet for anger and frustration? Norms form and younger officers learn the police way of doing things. Aversiveness festers and the gaps between individuals start to widen. Police officers absolutely detest this form of communication, it is controlling and unnecessary and it is not supporting.

Recent research by University of Illinois Professor Dolores Albarracin and Visiting Assistant Professor Ibrahim Senay, along with Kenji Noguchi, Assistant Professor at Southern Mississippi University, has shown that those who ask themselves whether they will perform a task generally do better than those who tell themselves that they will. Little research exists in the area of self-talk, although we are aware of an inner voice in ourselves and in literature.

Research like this challenges traditional paradigms regarding public service messages and self-help literature designed to motivate people toward healthier or more productive behaviour. The popular idea is that self-affirmations enhance people's ability to meet their goals. It seems, however, that when it comes to performing a specific behaviour, asking questions is a more promising way of achieving your objectives. Adding a little humour also helps people conform to working practices.

Asking questions as opposed to telling people what to do ensures compliance

PC Homes comments:

"I walked into my old station last week and noticed a new sign on the door 'Sgt Davies, deputy divisional commander'. Now, call me old-fashioned, but don't most of us know one another? The public are rarely allowed to enter past the front desk. The purpose of the sign is to inform newcomers to a part of the building that they are unfamiliar with. However, I think that Sgt Davies may need to remember his name and title every once and a while, just like the posters he displays each week, informing officers to 'wash their hands'. The real issue here is one of territorial positioning and it is one of the biggest reasons for reducing team effectiveness. Such practices are common but absolutely not needed, invisible psychological barriers are already in place, defensiveness begins. Does Sgt Davies need his name on the door? Does it serve a purpose or is it an opportunity for him to create his own home? In contrast, the CID office upstairs has a tuck shop, water cooler, air-conditioning, open office space and bright and breezy windows. There are no opportunities for physical and psychological barriers. The atmosphere is jovial and down to earth, a world apart from our dirty parade room. No posters on the wall, pictures of happy police officers taking part in golfing days and charity events. Morale on the CID is very high and it should be. There is a saying 'my door is always open'. Why have doors in the first place?

Reduce physical barriers

A more productive working environment

Many recent studies on job satisfaction have shown that workers who spend longer hours in office environments, often under artificial light in windowless offices, report reduced job satisfaction and increased stress levels.

How can employers make office environments more conducive to productivity and employee happiness? Try adding some 'green' to your office. Not greenbacks – green plants! A research study published in the February 2008 issue of 'HortScience' offers employers and corporations some valuable advice for upping levels of employee satisfaction by introducing simple measures.

Employees who worked in offices with windows and views of green spaces, and workers who had green plants in their offices perceived greater job satisfaction than employees who did not have access to these environmental components.

Paint the walls light, soothing greens and introduce some easy-to-look-after ferns

Research carried out at the Surrey Sleep Centre, at the University of Surrey in partnership with Philips Lighting, has revealed that changing traditional white-light lighting to blue-enriched white light helped office workers stay more alert and less sleepy during the day. The research also showed improvements in subjective measures of positive moods, work performance, fatigue in the evening, irritability, ability to concentrate and focus and eye strain. Furthermore, the workers reported improved sleep at night. The blue-enriched white light is thought to be more effective because it targets a recently discovered novel photoreceptor in the eye. **Change the lighting of the room and introduce blue light. Introduce some aromatherapy smells.**

Music

Music in its simplicity has shown to improve mood, concentration and well-being. Many police officers spend time in police vehicles and music can really help improve mood and thought during a busy shift. Police vehicles can be adapted to fit Bluetooth devices that allow officers to play their favourite songs.

Support boards

The police station should have a distinctive staff area that informs staff about the support that is available to them. Each board would be further broken down into areas of support that include:

Training – This board would include free courses available, up-and-coming training events. Details of officers with specialist knowledge in areas of drugs, domestic violence, etc. Police services could offer mentoring schemes to all staff, so that every member of staff throughout their career is paired up with a mentor. There is a wealth of experience within the workplace. Why not offer a master class on the subject of house searches or obtaining a warrant? Ask every department within the station to offer a monthly master class, so that we can share the best information. The crossover of various departments will serve to help every officer.

Expression board – This board will allow communication to flourish. Share a joke or funny tale with colleagues or place a well-known quote on the board. Ask a question and get an answer.

Support board – Add the details of health and fitness agencies, provide links to counselling and trauma therapy. Add details of events and pastimes. Offer alternative therapies or pieces of research. Add good news stories and letters of thanks.

Rumour board – If there are rumours spreading across the station, update the board and dispel them.

Try not to bamboozle staff with graphs, performance statistics and 'could do better' slogans, there is no evidence that this management practice improves morale or performance.

Breathing space

Not giving people breathing space when a serious matter has occurred has a detrimental effect. During extreme states of emotion and stress, our body's immune system works less efficiently. Scientific studies conducted on medical students during exam time show unequivocal responses to reduced immuno-response. Repeated exposure to stress has a long-term negative effect on the mind / body system. Supervisors monitor workload allocation on a daily basis, within this process allocation to stressful events should be monitored and shared amongst staff members. **Emotional rest during a shift period could be given to the police officer and not at the discretion of the supervisor.**

Single crewed vs. double crewed

"We must improve police visibility within our communities, when the public see us they feel safe and more confident; to that end, I want to see all officers single crewed and working alone."

Why do chief officers make decisions based on one piece of statistical information? Surely it would be better to make a decision based on a whole variety of factors. Police officers come across some of the most vulnerable people within society, officers can face a mountain of false allegations and this can be a very stressful experience. Searching suspects is better done with two, attending a crime scene is better with two, morale is better with two and the skills of an 'ethical observer' are best played by two. Impact factors, such as officer presence and dealing with confrontation, are best with two. You cannot support one another when you are working alone. Single crewed police officers do improve public confidence and the perception of safety. However, this can only be achieved when demand is low and staff resources are high. When adopting this working practice, there needs to be low current demands and intelligence that supports this idea.

Control

How much say the person has in the way they do their work

The standard is that:

- ❑ employees indicate that they are able to have a say about the way they do their work systems are in place locally to respond to any individual concerns;

- ❑ where possible, employees have control over their pace of work;

- ❑ employees are encouraged to use their skills and initiative to do their work;

- ❑ where possible, employees are encouraged to develop new skills to help them undertake new and challenging pieces of work;

- ❑ the organisation encourages employees to develop their skills;

- ❑ employees have a say over when breaks can be taken; and

- ❑ employees are consulted over their work patterns.

The very nature of police work involves control. We use our legal powers to control chaotic and violent individuals so that the public can have a safer, happier, peaceful experience. Within the service, control and power are constant struggles between serving officers and police managers. Many police managers are not aware of surface tension that surrounds control. It is an issue that surrounds the police locker room. However, for all the moans and groans about 'control' there has to be 'optimal control for managers and employees'. Frontline officers complain about the infringement of the policing role on the officers' personal and social life. Police Managers also have this issue to contend with and the extra responsibility to provide enough resources on any given day. It is a difficult issue to contend with from both perspectives, and compromise and communication is the only way forward. This issue is un-comparable to other organisations as control (in a policing sense) is an issue that is unique to the police.

Explaining negative control

PC Martin says:

"My current supervisor consistently checks up on me. Every incident is monitored and commented on. Whenever I start a piece of work, he will change the goal posts and ask me to do something else. When I don't complete the first task he has sent me, he asks me why I have failed his tasks. I never get left alone to do my work or use my own initiative. I am always treading on eggshells and being in is presence worries me. I have thought long and hard about his behaviour and style of management. I have realised that central to his style of management is the issue of trust and suspicion. He doesn't trust anyone and is suspicious of almost everyone. It is these personality traits that govern his management style."

PC David says:

"It's been really tough for us in the last three years, there are only four team members on my shift and my opportunities for day-to-day development have waned. I feel like I am treading on eggshells when I ask the Inspector for time off or even a meal break. It's such a huge issue, I asked to go on an attachment to the drugs squad and the intelligence department, but that was turned down. It's difficult to get time off and weekends are a no go. I wanted to go back to university and study forensics, but that was turned down. Often I ask the same questions: Can I go home early and take some time off? Can I have a meal break? Can I revise for my exams? Can I have a secondment? Can I have some leave, I am feeling stressed? The answer is predominately 'no'. I can't blame the Inspector as she doesn't have any time either. It's difficult to ask for help in taking statements and case building, everyone is busy."

The police service cannot realistically offer flexible working control if the frontline is seriously depleted, and that is a fact.

Explaining positive control

Senior Officer Smith says:

"I am torn between two rocks; I have to get enough resources together to make sure that you can have adequate meal breaks, protection, demands of the day, health and safety consideration and staffing issues. It may seem that you are being asked to contribute too much; however, control is administered to ensure that you are all supported when you come on duty, that's the distinctive difference. Without control of the workforce, I am effectively allowing certain shifts to increase in case workload and effectively increasing the stress levels of your colleagues."

	Police Officer	Police Supervisor	Senior Officer
Personal management style	Discusses issues with supervisor in a fair manner	Discusses staff issues with all members of staff	Discusses staff issues with all members of staff
	Is comfortable within staff circles	Is comfortable within staff circles	Is comfortable within staff circles
	Avoids spreading rumours if not happy with outcomes	Is fair and honest	Is fair and honest
		Doesn't raise expectations	Doesn't raise expectations
		A problem solver	A problem solver
		Makes allowances	Makes allowances
		Explains decisions and rationale behind them	Explains decisions and rationale behind them
		Allows staff to set some of the rules concerning leave, time off, work patterns, etc	Allows staff to set some of the rules concerning leave, time off, work patterns, etc
		Gives a certain amount of control to staff members an effective delegator and coach	Gives a certain amount of control to staff members an effective delegator and coach
Communication	Introduces You Said, We Did Communication styles across all departments	Introduces You Said, We Did Communication styles across all departments	Introduces You Said, We Did Communication styles across all departments
Annual leave	Plans time off according to own time and the organisation's needs	Allows staff to set some of the rules concerning leave, time off, work patterns, etc	Allows staff to set some of the rules concerning leave, time off, work patterns, etc
		Gets the balance of rest vs. demand across the working year. Adopts a flexible approach	Gets the balance of rest vs. demand across the working year. Adopts a flexible approach

	Police Officer	Police Supervisor	Senior Officer
Meal breaks	Plans and prepares for policing eventualities, e.g., food on the go, dried foods at the station	Organises and co-ordinates meal times. Allows discussion around the briefing table	
Work patterns	Allows staff to set some of the rules concerning leave, time off, work patterns, etc Discusses with all staff members current needs, e.g., Late finish due to childcare arrangements	Allows staff to set some of the rules concerning leave, time off, work patterns, etc Practices give and take, "Take some time off next week, you worked overtime recently"	Allows staff to set some of the rules concerning leave, time off, work patterns, etc Practices give and take, "Take some time off next week, you worked overtime recently"
Workload	Follows the URGENT and IMPORTANT model of workload management	Listens to the officer's URGENT and IMPORTANT case, avoids imposing further demand by adding other tasks or crime enquiries	Respects the officer's URGENT and IMPORTANT case, avoids imposing further demand by adding other tasks or crime enquiries

Relationships

Includes promoting positive working relationships to avoid conflict and dealing with unacceptable behaviour

The standard is that:

❏ employees indicate that they are not subjected to unacceptable behaviours, e.g., bullying at work; and

❏ the organisation promotes positive behaviours at work to avoid conflict and ensure fairness.

When we are stressed, our relationships become tense, by applying all the principles within this book, the necessary conditions for harmony within our relationships can begin to flourish. Traditionally, the police service uses sanctions, staff movement, confidential integrity lines, support systems and workforce mediation to try and improve staff relationships. This human resource perspective is usually a knee-jerk reaction to staff issues and doesn't address the perspective of 'systems thinking'. These policies are needed, but investing in our inner relationship and our outer relationship with others creates the foundation for equality and harmony to exist. Prevention as opposed to intervention.

To consider your work relationship with others, it may be useful to think about the qualities that you admire in others. There must be a member of staff that gets on with everyone and floats around the office with effortless ease. What does this person do? How do they make you feel? If we take on the good qualities of others, we are likely to positively affect others around us. Positive individuals magnetise others and create a 'can do' attitude. Relationships begin with the individual and by adopting some of the strategies within this book, your start to reduction in stress will undoubtedly spill over to improving your relationships at work.

Work on yourself first

Be true to yourself

"Your relationships can only be as healthy as you are." – Nick Clark Warren

Show who you really are, your unique self. Do not try to impress by being anybody but yourself. Always do your best at being yourself. Let your actions come out of who you really are, what you truly believe in, and the things you are devoted to. The prerequisite for relationship building is trust. Trust is built when people believe who you represent yourself to be.

Be honest

"Say what you'll do, and do what you say."

Don't make promises you can't keep and don't create expectations you can't fulfil. Avoid over-representing and overpromising. Be a man, woman or organisation of your word. That's integrity. As mentioned earlier, relationships are built with trust. And trust is built with belief in another person's integrity. Show integrity in your words and actions. That's the foundation of a good relationship.

Smile often

"The expression one wears on one's face is far more important than the clothes one wears on one's back."

Try walking in the street and observe people, what do you see? Is it a stressed, tired, irritated and impatient expression? Or is it enthusiastic, heart-warming and real smile of people? One of the diseases of this career-driven world is that we get too serious with ourselves that we forget to wear the most important outfit in our life, our smile.

A smile says, "I like you. You make me happy. I am glad to see you".

If you want to start attracting and creating good relationships with people, start by walking and greeting people with your most beautiful smile.

Stop criticising, condemning and complaining

"If you want to gather honey, don't kick over the beehive." – Dale Carnegie

By criticising, condemning and complaining, it does not change a situation, oftentimes, it only creates more problems, such as resentment and broken relationships. Instead of criticising, condemning and complaining against others, why not try to understand them? Put yourself in their situation or try to figure out how to move forward with the solution. That's a lot more helpful and gainful than criticism and complaining, which often doesn't solve anything.

No one is perfect, and I'm pretty sure you are not as well, even though we often think we are always right. It is human nature to blame, criticise and judge the actions of others except our own. We are not perfect ourselves to even judge others. If you want to change and improve your relationship with people in your environment, begin in yourself. It's more easier and a lot less dangerous than trying to improve others.

Be genuinely interested in other people

"It may be true that interesting people attract attention, but I believe that interested people attract appreciation." – Mark Sanborn

You can make more friends in two months by becoming genuinely interested in other people than you can in two years of trying to get people interested on you. People are not interested in you, they are not interested in me. They are interested in themselves – morning, noon and after dinner.

As such, if you want to build good relationships with other people, you have to become interested with their favourite person, themselves. People are pleased when you put an interest in getting to know them better, not out of bad curiosity, but in an effort to build relationships. So the next time you want to build a relationship with a stranger, instead of boasting your accomplishments and declaring your great self, try to be more interested in the story of the stranger. You will not only gain a new friend, but also lots of new knowledge and wisdom.

Consider others' wants and interests

"It is the individual who is not interested in his fellow men who has the greatest difficulties in life and provides the greatest injury to others." – Alfred Adler

To better illustrate this, I'll share with you a scenario I've personally encountered. I'm a person who wasn't raised and trained in dealing with other people. In our family, children are given the most priority, that's why I was becoming a bit bratty and selfish when I was growing up. I brought this bratty and selfish attitude into school and aroused difficult situations with other people.

To cut the story short, when I slowly realised that my attitude wasn't helping me build relationship with others, I started to realise that happy and harmonious relationships with other people begins with me. It begins when I start to become interested in other people's welfare, wants and interests, not solely of my own. I've learned to adjust and be flexible with the people I deal with instead of complaining and criticising the other person then trying to change them for me. When I started to become more selfless, that's when I started to gain true happiness, unity, teamwork and friendship with other people.

Treat people with importance and respect

"The life of many person would probably be changed if only someone would make him feel important." – Ronald Rowland

Almost everyone considers themselves important, very important. The truth is that almost everyone you meet feels to themselves that they are superior to you in some way. And a way to build a good relationship with this kind of person is to recognise their importance and be sincere with it. Once you sincerely believe that every man you meet is superior to you in some way, you will learn more from each person you meet. Always make other people feel important. It is human nature to crave appreciation.

Be generous in giving sincere appreciation and praise

"Try leaving a friendly trail of little sparks of gratitude on your daily trips." – Dale Carnegie

One of the most neglected virtues of our daily activity is appreciation. A simple "thank you" to the guard who opened the gate for you, or the small gesture of your assistant who prepared a cup of coffee for you. Showing a sincere appreciation and praise can change a person's life. It can boost another person's self-esteem, confidence and enthusiasm to bring out much greater value.

On the other hand, lack of appreciation and praise results to make other person feel insecure, unappreciated or invalid.

Begin creating positive relationships and environments by being generous in praising and appreciating others. Remember, small acts when accumulated creates big difference.

Be a good listener rather than a good talker

"People who talk only of themselves think only of themselves. And those people who think only of themselves, are hopeless uneducated. They are not educated, no matter how instructed they may be." – Dr. Nicholas Murray Butler

Have you ever been in a conversation with someone wherein you have been talking about something then suddenly the other person cuts in and tell his story? What did you feel? What about having a conversation to someone who was talking to you about something, but instead of listening attentively, even before he finished his speech, you are already thinking your response.

Being a good listener in our time now is a real talent. Everyone is too busy and too pre-occupied with their own life that they lack time to listen. But if you want to really create a big, positive change in your life and build good relationships with other people, you have to learn how to become a good sincere listener. Be genuinely interested with other people's lives.

Get to know your colleagues

Getting to know the aptitudes, skills and abilities of all staff is a very important step.

Police officers have not always been police officers and may have a range of skills. Recently the commander spent thousands on an outside company to build a new website. This process costs thousands of pounds. If the commander had done his homework, he would have realised that three police officers in his station were qualified website designers.

Getting to know staff at a deeper level, can create many opportunities.

The power of rewarding staff

Personal achievements would have not been possible if it had not been for the amazing team members that we have had the privilege of working with. Award ceremonies should focus on the 'whole' and not its 'parts'. If the organisation has a 'success' notice board, be sure to recognise the bigger picture. Consider the following statements:

'Anti-social behaviour down by 20% when compared to last year, well done!'

Or

'Anti-social behaviour down by 20% when compared to last year, this is because: response officers have responded quicker and referred people directly to the anti-social behaviour co-ordinator, this has resulted in the local analyst

directing staff to hotspots and informing other partners about this issue. Youth

workers, substance misuse workers and truanting officers have been directed to these areas. The local community officer has identified a number of repeat

offenders and is currently applying for a set of crasbos. The licensing officer has made a case for an alcohol exclusion order and this has the full backing of the senior management team. Our partners at the local council have placed a CCTV camera at these locations. A huge thank you to all staff involved in making these areas safer and happier places to live. Mrs Jones, a local resident, has written to us and says thank you for all your hard work."

Remember everyone wants to feel important.

Improving relationships the power of food

The power of food has had a dramatic effect on Christian societies the world over. The last supper has been modelled and ritualised across all the continents. Indeed, in every society the 'get together' is a sign of a healthy and vibrant family. The giving and preparing of food is a sign of care and

attention, it nourishes and fosters a spirit of relationship. Food brings people together at a human level and offers opportunities for understanding and debate. Why not organise a station barbeque or use food as a gathering point?

Improving relationships: the power of sporting, family and charity events

Every year, in the old 'f' division calendar, a number of social gatherings occur.

An office lady at Porthcawl Police Station organises a superb family Christmas Day at the hi-tide public house. Every child has a Christmas present and it is a chance for old acquaintances to meet and relax. This was first started by PC Lyn Ingram and successively passed onto Alison Davies and her little elves.

The CID office regularly goes on charity events, last year they climbed the three peaks in aid of charity. And, lastly, and by no means least, the annual charity boxing match. Picture the scene, hundreds of spectators watching 10 bouts of quality boxing. Dinner jackets donned and cigars at the ready.

These events have a huge impact on the workplace atmosphere, they bind people together and foster a sense of community.

Improving relationships allowing humour to flourish

Why is laughter good for us? When we feel good in ourselves we are more likely to follow a healthy lifestyle, and you don't need me to tell you the benefits of this. Laughter can help to keep blood pressure in the safety zone by reducing stress such that someone is less likely to turn to unhealthy behaviours that increase blood pressure, such as drinking alcohol and eating sweet snacks, to help them unwind.

But it's not just about having fun. Laughter has real health benefits that go beyond lifting the spirits. Scientific research has identified that people with a healthy heart are more likely to laugh frequently than those people who have heart disease. It isn't clearly understood how laughing helps, but it is thought that laughing may cause a reduction in stress hormones and consequently a lowering of blood pressure.

Researchers in California found laughter reduces stress and enhances mood – something I think many of us are already aware of – but also reduces stress hormones, lowers blood pressure and levels of 'bad' cholesterol. Whilst a person watched comedy clips they found levels of hormones produced by moderate physical exercise, were increased. They've now called this 'laughtercise', seriously.

Improving Relationships	Police Officer	Police Supervisor	Senior Officer
Personal style	Be true to yourself	Be true to yourself	Be true to yourself
	Be honest	Be honest	Be honest
	Smile often	Smile often	Smile often

Improving Relationships	Police Officer	Police Supervisor	Senior Officer
Communication	Stop Criticising, condemning and complaining Be genuinely interested with other people Consider others' wants and interests Treat people with importance and respect Be a good listener rather than a good talker	Stop Criticising, condemning and complaining Be genuinely interested with other people Consider others' wants and interests Treat people with importance and respect Be a good listener rather than a good talker	Stop Criticising, condemning and complaining Be genuinely interested with other people Consider others' wants and interests Treat people with importance and respect Be a good listener rather than a good talker
Social events	Know your colleagues Improving relationships: the power of sporting, family and charity events	Know your staff members' personal history Support sporting, family and charity events	Know your staff members' personal history Support sporting, family and charity events
Laughter	Improving relationships allowing humour to flourish Tell some old tales or share a funny tale	Organise bring a joke 'day' or a story-telling hour. Bring some old photos or attend a fancy dress	Hire a comedian for a stand-up police comedy night Armed Forces have been using this practice for centuries! Support humour around the station and tell old war stories

Improving Relationships	Police Officer	Police Supervisor	Senior Officer
Rewarding staff	Be generous in giving sincere appreciation and praise The power of rewarding staff	Be generous in giving sincere appreciation and praise Involve the whole team and make use of commendations and award ceremonies	Have an annual service rewards ceremony
Reduce demoralising behaviour	Report inappropriate and unethical behaviour Avoid rumours spreading and report malicious rumours	Report inappropriate and unethical behaviour, address the root cause. Quash rumours at the earliest opportunity	Use a variety of approaches to address this issue Quash rumours at the earliest opportunity

Communication

During the summer period, senior officers engage in morale-boosting emails. The morale-boosting emails surface and all staff are told how great they are and what a fantastic job they are doing. If you are a senior officer reading this Paragraph, whatever you do, don't send that email!

Firing off emails and cueing up video conferences gets work done fast, but not necessarily well, research by a University of Illinois business leadership expert found. The study put more than 200 undergraduate students through two hypothetical teamwork exercises, some face-to-face and others through email and video conferences. Face-to-face contact yielded the most trust and cooperation while email netted the least, with video conferences somewhere in between. The study shows businesses need to re-examine their use of high-tech communication, which has grown over the last two decades because of its expediency and because more companies are spread out geographically rather than under the same roof. The key is recognising the limitations and recognising that exclusive reliance on these lean communications mediums can be potentially dangerous, or at least limiting. Findings suggest that businesses should balance use of email with face-to-face meetings to 'recharge' relationships and the trust they instil. When people meet face-to-face, they can leverage that over a pretty lean communication medium for a while and the relationship will not degrade. But, after a while, they need to get back together face-to-face to recharge the trust, the engagement and the loyalty in the relationship.

Should and blaming statements

Picture the scene, the morning shift is getting prepared for a busy summer shift. The sergeant hands out the remaining work that was handed over from the night shift. The night shift officers look tired and fed up. Each officer is given a number of incidents to attend to and there are six prisoners in the cells. The morning shift's demands are saturated to start with. All those plans that each officer has considered are now shattered. The shift, while attending the briefing, begins to sift through each file of evidence.

PC Gronow, whilst reading the handed-over file of evidence, makes the following observation:

"I can't believe what I am reading, they should have taken a statement, should have organised the CCTV to be viewed and should have written up some decent notes! What a lazy shift, they do this all the time, making more work for me."

PC Lewis adds to the conversation:

"They don't even do the basics, they never update incidents or make the correct decisions, this file should have had all the basics covered, but no, there is no excuse it was only 5am."

At every level, at every station, the fly on the wall tells the same story; police officers grumble, complain and ruminate about work colleagues, departments, managers, senior officers and the service in general. 'Should' statements are based in a virtual reality, where police officers conjure up the perfect scenario of how police work should be completed. 'Should' statements are absolute and are really no more than values and needs that are imposed on others. Police work is very procedural and policy orientated, and at its very core contains a great deal of 'should do's' or 'you will do'. It is the imposing of blind policy that creates a feeling of being over controlled.

PC Willmot has a meeting with her supervisor:

Supervisor: "I have reason to talk to you today about the submission of your poor file of evidence. I have major issues with your paperwork. Firstly, let me explain. You didn't take a statement at the earliest opportunity, why was this? When you did write the statement, it was only a small paragraph? It was very poor and had no detail. You didn't update the crime report or refer the victim to the appropriate agency. You know that you should take a detailed statement and immediately after the incident, you know that you should put far more detail into your statements and update the appropriate agency. Your actions have caused me to look like a poor supervisor and everyone is talking about how poor your work is, it reflects badly on me as your supervisor."

PC Willmot says: "The victim was concussed as a result of the assault and was visibly sick, she didn't make any sense after the incident and her words were incoherent. When she came into the station the next week, I formed the opinion that she had taken some type of drug, she was very anxious, kept on biting her nails and grinding her teeth. I made numerous attempts to calm her down, but nothing worked, she kept on saying that she wanted to leave the station. I was powerless and she said all that she wished to say. The victim ran out of the station. This is my explanation."

Supervisor: "How could you have done things different? What will you do next time? What do I want to hear?"

PC Willmot says: "I don't know what you mean? The situation was beyond my control."

Supervisor: "The next time you have to take a statement, you will follow force policy and you will do as it says in the manual of guidance, you will follow best practice. You will not let me down or yourself, is that understood?"

Does this sound familiar? 'Should' statements are based on the assumption that someone has violated appropriate rules of behaviour, the person who holds strong 'should' beliefs now faces a dilemma. The situation presents a right answer and a wrong answer. The supervisor splits responses into right and wrong and feels that they are justified in stating that PC Willmot is guilty of wrongdoing. The supervisor thinks that you are wrong and that this issue needs to be addressed by sanctions, action plans or disciplinary proceedings. The supervisor, in this case, hasn't considered the conditions presented by PC Willmot and has made a sweeping assumption that PC Willmot is incompetent. Ask yourself what does right or wrong mean to you? The supervisor has twisted the argument around to include a blaming statement.

There are two problems with 'should' assumption. Other people have their own definition of appropriate rules of conduct and this definition may differ from yours. Secondly, police officers are all too aware of what they should do, but the circumstances surrounding the incident require flexibility and making the best of a difficult situation. Police work is not black and white or right or wrong. Consider your approach from conditions, cause and effect and you may see that your whole perception could change.

In order to counteract such divisive thinking patterns, consider placing a reminder for all to see.

Consider the following statements and try to counteract the obstacle of rigid thinking.

"Police officers do what they are able to do in very stressful, demanding circumstances, not what I think they should do in the confines of a peaceful office."

"Should do's create a divisive workforce, they cause people to feel angry and reduce team morale, open communication is the key to helping one another."

"I may not like it, but the shift before me tried their best."

"Realise that different people have strengths and weaknesses."

'Should' statements also contain an element of entitlement and can create the belief of being deliberately deprived.

"This file of evidence doesn't contain a witness statement, they wanted to make it harder for me, it was a deliberate attempt to undermine me."

This type of language and thinking is the language of a victim. When we adopt the role of a victim, we create an element of unfairness.

"This is always happening to me, it is as if I am being targeted."

Unfortunately, no two people can agree on what is fair. Fairness is a subjective judgement that reflects a person's perception. Perception is constantly changing.

Consider the following statements and try to counteract the obstacle of fairness.
"Our needs are equally important."

"Nobody is right and nobody is wrong. We just have different needs."

"Each need is legitimate, we can negotiate."

Should statements within the policing context are supported by the belief that you can change people if you apply enough pressure. Unfortunately, people change only when they see it is in their interests to change and when they are capable of changing. No amount of threat, nagging or action planning will cause people to change if they don't want to. It is tough to accept that some people will sometimes fall below your standards, but it takes courage to support, foster and improve relationships with those officers who struggle a little.

Consider the following statements and try to counteract the obstacle of control.
"I accept that we are all different, nobody is inherently bad."

"While I don't agree, I am not going to waste my time trying to impose my way of doing things."

"People change when they are supported and when they realise that they need to change."

When we engage in blaming others for poor standards of work or increasing our workload, we create the trappings of an over-sensitive response to everyday situations. Blaming is easy and takes the responsibility away from us, our ability to respond is also hampered; we become stuck and create even more inner turmoil and anger. In order to make the best of a situation, we need to have the ability to choose our response and consider the appropriate remedy. Blaming always assumes the worst of a situation and we believe that the actions of others are deliberate. We don't know the motives of others, as we never ask them so, to silence the facts, we create a distortion. The distortion is what we believe they should do and why they have acted in such a way. While we create this distortion, it is usually mixed with resentment and anger. When did you last see the facts clearly in anger? Inner feelings such as anger and resentment colour the situation and we are literally blinded.

PC Davies turns and shouts across the room, "That bloody radio operator is not doing what I ask them, she always does this to me, it's because she has never been a police officer and hasn't a clue!"

Can PC Davies read the operator's mind? Is he making a large assumption? Is he second guessing the motives of others?

Consider the following statements and try to counteract the obstacle of blaming.

"Try not to second guess the motives of others."

"Test your assumptions."

"Try not to jump to conclusions and assume the worst."

"This is not personal."

'Should' and 'blaming' statements within the police writing room create the necessary conditions for procrastination and a reduction in work productivity. How many times have you heard yourself and your colleagues sit and pick holes in other's work and the service in general?

"If they think I am dealing with this, they gotta another think coming."

"If I were in charge, I would do such and such."

"It's always our department that are doing the work, why should we help them out?"

"I am going to the senior officer about this matter, enough is enough."

Remind yourself why work doesn't get done, 'should' and 'blaming' are always responsible in the absence of 'communication' and 'responsibility', that means you, and only you. The official 'moanathon' that police officers are party to, should be encouraged, distinct opportunities for growth, communication and problem solving exist. 'Moanathons' can be used to improve morale and staff working arrangements. Don't bury your grumbles but come to the table with your problems and, most importantly, the solution to the issue that is bothering you.

You said, we did

Partnerships and Communities Together (PACT) meetings signified a cultural change within the UK police service. Members of the public, for the first time, had a sense of ownership and the power to direct police officers to areas of community concern. After the meeting, the police and partners had to agree three local priorities that were Specific, Measurable, Achievable, Realistic and Timely. Once those priorities were set and achieved the public were given the good news. You said and we did. This cultural shift signified enhanced listening, consent, trust and confidence.

Whilst I chaired a PACT meeting for five years, I noticed that my relationship with my community began to change. If I asked for support, help or advice, it was delivered, no questions asked. My ability to listen and act gave me the ability to achieve even more objectives. The local community treated me as I had treated them. A two-way relationship began to develop. You said and we did was echoed across all community levels.

This experience and its guiding principle could be emulated across the police workforce and at all levels. Police officers who are given the opportunity to comment could, in effect, set a number of priorities for police managers and vice versa. Imagine a police station where on the wall were set a number of monthly staff priorities that each and every department and rank structure had discussed and achieved. Morale and communication would surely improve, control would be undermined.

Police Officer	Police Supervisor	Senior Officer
You said (Police Supervisor)	**(Police Officer) You said**	**You said (Police Supervisor)**
1. Improve Intelligence Reports	1. Need a new photocopier	1. Need better evidence kits
2. Increase drink drivers arrests	2. Need to discuss shift patterns	2. More resources
3. Attend training	3. Improve interview room	3. Provide rape-trained officers
We did (Police Officer)	**We did (Police Supervisor)**	**We did (Senior Officer)**
1. All the above	1. Installed photocopier	1. Ordered new evidence kits
2.	2. Offered alternatives	2. Gave an extra resource
3.	3. Ordered new furniture	3. Organised training

Culturally, this form of engagement, consultation and action will signify an internal change within the police service. Norms and habits form and this will in turn allow us to engage more effectively with our communities. A change from the inside signifies change from the outside.

Role

Whether people understand their role within the organisation and whether the organisation ensures that the person does not have conflicting roles.

The standard is that:

❑ employees indicate that they understand their role and responsibilities; and

❑ systems are in place locally to respond to any individual concerns. What should be happening/states to be achieved:

❑ the organisation ensures that, as far as possible, the different requirements it places upon employees are compatible;

❑ the organisation provides information to enable employees to understand their role and responsibilities.

When I spoke to police officers about the conflict of 'role', the overwhelming response was that of hitting a brick wall. The job of the frontline police officer is particularly confusing and doesn't have a defining role and this is the reason why it can become frustrating. We are sometimes called to many roles and this doesn't have to be from a negative perspective or indeed frustrating. The job of the police officer actually develops its staff in many ways. These skills develop over time and enhance the workforce, although there is no qualifying piece of paper at the end of the year, development has most definitely taken place. Read through your pocket notebook for the period of an entire year. Consider all the incidents that you have attended, the highs, the lows, the laughter and the danger. A rollercoaster of emotions and many opportunities for role development. Police officers are like chameleons, adapting and changing to the incidents demands and needs. Over the past couple of years, how many roles have you adopted?

Undertaker, counsellor, teacher, administrator, presenter, cleaner, friend, legal aid, manager, first aider, lifeguard, driver, shepherd, midwife, pastor, protector, taxi driver, social worker, social engineer, leader, spy, negotiator, mediator, investigator, human rights activist and police officer.

Personally, 'role' can be somewhat frustrating, but just looking at our role from a different perspective can give us an indication of how unique and special it is to be able to contribute in the way that we do. It is frustrating, but in our personal frustration there is growth and development. This standard is applicable to police officers when our demands are being pulled from different sources; an example being a police officer who has been given extra responsibilities, such as mentoring, training, managing and numerous special projects. When demand is intertwined with a conflicting and unachievable role, the conditions for a stressful outcome magnify.

Change

How organisational change (large or small) is managed and communicated in the organisation.

The standard is that:

❑ employees indicate that the organisation engages them frequently when undergoing an organisational change; and

❑ systems are in place locally to respond to any individual concerns. What should be happening/states to be achieved:

- the organisation provides employees with timely information to enable them to understand the reasons for proposed changes;

- the organisation ensures adequate employee consultation on changes and provides opportunities for employees to influence proposals;

- employees are aware of the probable impact of any changes to their jobs. If necessary, employees are given training to support any changes in their jobs;

- employees are aware of timetables for changes.

'Change happens, so let's just get on with it'. Let's be honest, not everyone likes change. Many books and theories have been written about change management and it seems that introducing change can be uncomfortable for many staff members. The police service is a highly responsive organisation and change happens on a daily basis. How do we all adapt to this inevitable process? There are a number of well-researched theories and simple techniques that can be administered at all levels. Personal, group, shift and organisational change begins with a number of questions.

Identify the problem

What is the problem? What do we need to change? Why do we need to change?

Take the problem to the bottom floor

Staff know the answers to all the change problems. Managers have the responsibility to skilfully facilitate and enable change. The manager's role is to interpret, communicate and enable – not to instruct and impose, which nobody really responds to well. Check that people affected by the change agree with, or at least understand, the need for change, and have a chance to decide how the change will be managed, and to be involved in the planning and implementation of the change. Use face-to-face communications to handle sensitive aspects of organisational change management. Email and written notices are extremely weak at conveying and developing understanding.

Don't sell change, let the bottom floor do the talking and thinking

'Selling' change to people is not a sustainable strategy for success. When people listen to a management high-up 'selling' them a change, decent, diligent folk will generally smile and appear to accede, but quietly to themselves, they are thinking, "No bloody chance mate, if you think I'm standing for that load of old bollocks you've another think coming..." (And that's just the amenable types – the other more recalcitrant types will be well on the way to making their own particular transition from gamekeepers to poachers.)

Think emotions

John Fisher, an expert in the field of personal change, identified an emotional transition curve that explains people's emotional responses. Counteracting our emotional drives is a sure way of matching needs and winning change.

Anxiety – Individuals are unable to picture the future and this creates anxiety.

Happiness – Individuals feel a relief that things are going to change and not continue.

Fear – Individuals will need to act in a differing manner and this alters the person's self-perception, which can induce threat to the person.

If these emotional drives are not prepared for, depression, disillusionment, hostility and denial can be the predominating states of mind. A successful manager recognises the need to talk openly about the emotional drives by asking questions. What are your fears and worries? How will this change affect all of us? Once these fears are on the 'table', it is important to answer these issues with honesty.

Avoid imposing

Whenever an organisation imposes new things on people there will be difficulties. Participation, involvement and open, early, full communication are the important factors.

Workshops are very useful processes to develop collective understanding, approaches, policies, methods, systems, ideas, etc. Staff surveys are a helpful way to repair damage and mistrust among staff – provided you allow people to complete them anonymously, and provided you publish and act on the findings. Communicate in a 'you said, we did' style.

Change	Police Officer	Police Supervisor	Senior Officer
	Identify your inner barriers to change. Work out your fears and worries	Identify your inner barriers to change. Work out your fears and worries	Identify your inner barriers to change. Work out your fears and worries
	Formulate a number of questions and give them to your supervisor	Formulate a number of questions and give them to your supervisor	Understand your staff members' fears and worries
	Be open to consultation, take an active part in its development	Understand your staff members fears and worries	
	Avoid spreading gossip and rumours	Organise a forum, workshop and disseminate a staff questionnaire	Organise a forum, workshop and disseminate a staff questionnaire
	Report rumours to your supervisor	Be available to answer questions in person, avoid email and written communication	Be available to answer questions in person, avoid email and written communication
		Avoid imposing or saying "tough, get on with it"	Avoid imposing or saying "tough, get on with it"
		Avoid close door management meetings, if necessary publish management minutes	Avoid close door management meetings, if necessary publish those minutes
		Incorporate change and rumour boards, informing staff at all times	Incorporate change and rumour boards, informing staff at all times

7

ETHICAL POLICING

Ethics: moral principles that govern a person's behaviour or the conducting of an activity.

Schools of ethics in Western philosophy can be divided, very roughly, into three sorts. The first, drawing on the work of Aristotle, holds that the virtues (such as justice, charity, and generosity) are dispositions to act in ways that benefit both the person possessing them and that person's society. The second, defended particularly by Kant, makes the concept of duty central to morality: humans are bound, from a knowledge of their duty as rational beings, to obey the categorical imperative to respect other rational beings. Thirdly, utilitarianism asserts that the guiding principle of conduct should be the greatest happiness or benefit of the greatest number.

Whether we think about ethics or have rarely considered our actions, our decisions fall within two distinct needs. We strive for sensory happiness and do our very best to avoid suffering. When we wake in the morning, we go to the bathroom and, from habit, wash, bathe and brush our teeth. Depending on our motivation we wash and beautify ourselves for three distinct reasons. If we didn't wash and clean ourselves our susceptibility to infection, disease and illness increases. We create the conditions for future pain and suffering. By contrast, if our motivation is different, our routine of washing, allows our body to smell fragranced and clean, giving ourselves and others the benefit of a clean and fresh aroma. It could be said that our motivation was to induce a subtle form of sensory happiness for ourselves and others to benefit from. The third reasoning, being simple habit, we do what we were told to do. Our motivation is neutral. The application of this rationale can be applied to many aspects of our lives, the clothes we wear, the food we choose to eat, the work we engage in, our hobbies and past times, the friendships we form and the financial decisions we make. At a subconscious level, we are sometimes aware of what activities can bring about sensory happiness and a certain amount of discomfort and suffering. I refer to happiness as 'sensory happiness'. I am referring to the sensory experience of touch, taste, sight, smell, sound and the relationship that sound, smell and images have on our inner feelings and general well-being.

As human beings, we bathe in our senses, we have all experienced how seemingly enjoyable experiences begin to change and possibly raise discomfort in our hearts and minds.

The sound of your favourite music artist at first becomes enjoyable, but after time, the sound and feeling become a little boring. Chocolate and its consumption seems to feel and taste luxurious, but after indulging in more and more, our appetite changes. We feel sick and repulsed by its very sight. The feeling of our first romantic encounter, from excitement to adventure, eventually changes to a more even and balanced feeling. The sight of a new experience, but after time it registers as always being the same.

Exercise 1

Reflect on your weekly activities and identify where your motivations come from. Are you searching for an experience? Are you doing what you were told to do or merely avoiding unpleasant activities. This exercise will pull you out of your current ingrained habits and help you identify opportunities for inner development. By learning about the activities that we avoid or secretly crave, we can begin to understand the emotional temptations that have more attraction or repulsion. **We sometimes are unaware of our habits.**

Activity	Attracted / Rewarded	Repulsion / Avoidance
Shopping		
Confrontation		
Drinking alcohol		
Dating		
New relationships		
Making money		
Being important 'adopting a role'		

How do we become automatic in our ethical responses?

Eastern Ethical approaches place more emphasis on the individuals mind and the interaction with feelings and mindful intention. The outcomes of ethical conduct are a by-product of the thinking mind; therefore it is the way in which we think, feel and act that is of paramount importance. We may appear to be making progress, but this appearance can be deceptive. Whilst we were growing up, we were probably introduced to a simple form of ethics by the use of reward or punishment. If we showed positive behaviour we were usually rewarded. For example, if we ate our food, went to sleep, spoke nicely to our parents, shared our sweets we were usually given a reward for such good behaviour. This type of conditioning is evident across many schools today and it is perceived as a successful way of allowing young children to understand rule setting, standards and general etiquette.

Rewards are followed with positive affirmations: *"You were such a good boy."*

You cleaned your teeth: *"That's good."*

You listened: *"That's good."*

You share with others: *"That's good."*

You passed your exams: *"That's good."*

You had a wash: *"That's good."*

Notice that everyday activities have 'good' affirmations. With such obvious labelling does the word 'good' have meaning in different circumstances? Looking at the list above, the only activity that has a moral intention is that of sharing. Cleaning your teeth is of no ethical concern. Both activities were given the label 'good'. Based on this small example, rules and the dividing line between 'good' and 'bad' start to form.

Does the word 'good' have a feeling? Do those feelings change in different circumstances? Is the word 'good' a suitable word for this inner feeling?

Similarly, when we broke the code, rule, standard or law, we were given an appropriate punishment. Affirmations such as "You're naughty" or "Bad child" were placed upon us. Some families use fear as a tactic, for example, taking away a privilege, threatening to do something horrible or even using a slap as physical punishment. Now suppose that you stole something because you were hungry, the consequences of being caught were always met with physical punishment. You always had a 'back hand'. The fear of being hit, did not stop you from actually stealing, it was ineffective. Now suppose you got caught red-handed. Are you honestly going to tell the truth? You know that even if you tell the truth, you're still going to be physically punished. Would it be OK to limit your story, perhaps to blame someone else? Lessen the blow and save your skin? Fear doesn't promote honesty, in fact it can support the habit of dishonesty.

In the first exercise, I asked you to consider what personal activities gave rise to wanting an experience or avoiding an experience. Reward and punishment strengthen those inner drives of wanting or avoiding. Whilst we engage with this idea, we create habits.

Reward and punishment eventually bypass our inner drives and we can become confused as to what is morally correct or merely an effort to place control over someone. Imagine living in a world where everything that we say or do is judged as good or bad? Is this a happy world or is it rigid, controlling and stressful?

As the good child encounters experiences that differ from his/her set of rules or good affirmations, a predictable response emerges. When the child sees or experiences an opposing set of circumstances the term 'bad' resonates. The word 'bad' moves into a whole myriad of feelings. Feelings that we don't like, and compel us to act in ways that foster aversion, blame and denial. Our view imposes on others and our behaviour changes.

That person is fat: *"That's bad."*

That person doesn't have clean shoes: *"That's bad."*

That person hasn't combed her hair: *"That's bad."*

Notice that everyday activities have 'bad' affirmations. With such obvious labelling does the word 'bad' have meaning in different circumstances? Does the word 'bad' have a feeling? Do those feelings change in different circumstances? Is the word 'bad' a suitable word for this inner feeling?

There are a number of associated problems with this approach. Firstly, when you don't get rewarded, how do you feel? Do you feel upset and rejected, annoyed and unsupported? Secondly, when someone doesn't behave according to your set of rules? How do you react to them, is it with kindness and openheartedness or is it with frustration? Once inner frustration sets in, how do you react? Do you scowl at the other person and gossip about them? Do you feel angry and upset? Does your behaviour change? Do you simmer with rage?

This process is called 'splitting' and it is a process that labels everyday activities into 'good' or 'bad' and sets up the conditions for a judgemental, rigid and unethical response to everyday situations. Where this approach falters is that it doesn't develop a coping mechanism or technique when life becomes challenging. When someone hurts us or says something we do not like we say "He/she is a bad person!" We project our inner feelings onto that person and make them faulty. We do this because we identify with the idea of 'bad'. We know that 'bad' always with links with 'punishment'. So we decide to punish the other person or make a judgement. Rewarding 'good' behaviour is a short-term solution, but, in the long term, we are not learning to cope and tackle negative states of mind, such as anger, jealousy and malice. We are not placing ourselves in a position of flexibility; we are not attempting to see the situation from a balanced perspective. We are being conditioned into moving towards the reward. The valuable inner experience is being overlooked and it is this inner experience that compels us to act in unwholesome ways.

The third problem is our intention. Did we act with the intention to benefit others, with compassion and understanding? Or did we act to achieve an objective? The objective of getting a reward of some kind. This type of ethical exchange becomes a form of bartering. We will only be nice to someone if there is something at the end of the exchange or I will act with kindness because someone else may think that I am a good person. Our expectation of reward actually interferes with the process of giving and our true altruistic intention. Our habitual way of ethics is so mixed up with reward and can be very difficult to see. If we acted with pure altruistic intention, do you think we would feel let down by others? Would we feel frustrated if we didn't get a reward? Reward bypasses inner feelings of giving and generosity.

I am not saying that reward and punishment are not suitable in certain situations, for example, a child being punished for hitting another child or being rewarded for sharing with others. Where the confusion and conditioning interlink is when this ethical process is used in every single daily situation and the pairing of this process with the words or rules of 'good' and 'bad'. **When we really consider this approach, we begin to realise that our actions are usually automatic, we move to the 'reward' or avoid 'punishment', but in this process we bypass ethical awareness and our true inner intention, in effect our values.**

Policing rarely deals with the 'good', it mostly deals with the 'bad'. In previous chapters, I talked about the process of 'values frustration' and how the build-up of this process can lead to changes of perception and, ultimately, behaviour. Whilst values frustration begins to snowball after years and years of policing, cynicism, mistrust, anger and control can begin to become the predominate states of mind. We support our habits. Coincidentally, attitudes and behavioural characteristics generated by police work itself can lead to rigidity, suspiciousness, cynicism and authoritarianism, which are attributed to burnout.

Once we have identified our conditioned way of thinking, we turn inwards and literally watch our minds, this is mindfulness.

Eastern approaches to ethical conduct begin from the heart, intention translates into action and the by-product or the reward is of no importance. Although we strive for sensory happiness and do our best to avoid dissatisfaction, it is our intention that guides us from the very outset. In your day-to-day role, ask yourself what is your intention. The reward and punishment thinking process literally spills over into the policing culture.

Are you making an arrest to improve your performance statistics?

Are you listening to what the public want?

Are you publicising your success no matter what?

Are you concealing the truth and cutting corners because you want a result?

Having you identified ways of helping others, are you ignoring these opportunities?

Do you frequently argue with staff and make in-house moves?

Do you treat the 'bad' people fairly?

Are you acting in a certain way, so that you are readily accepted by your new team?

Are you revising for your exams to improve your knowledge or do you want the lure of a new title or more money?

Are you building your profile for your own means and are you doing this for future promotion?

Do you feel frustrated most of the time?

Are you making decisions just in case someone criticises you? Are you scared of criticism? Is criticism an anxious feeling? How often do you think about benefiting others? Is your career the only aspect of your life you think about?

How do our habits interfere with our policing role?
Thinking about the work of the frontline police officer, does the job accrue rewards on a daily basis? Is there a good story at the end? Do we sometimes expect a reward or some form of justice? You may find that your expectation is greater than the

rewards of daily policing, and therein lies a source of inner frustration. We look at court cases, commendations, letters of thanks and expect some form of reward. But, if we are truly honest with ourselves, our efforts are rarely considered most of the time. **Police work requires the understanding of ethical decision making as it is this guiding principle that determines so much of what we do on a daily basis.** If our intention is unbiased, we experience day-to-day policing as a process, instead of a bumpy ride.

With respect to policing decisions, the rewards culture can be easily seen. Instead of charging a prolific burglar with a string of offences, we cheat and offer bail and detect a number of crimes via offences taken into consideration. We let the one-man crime wave out onto the streets and even more crime is committed. Why does this happen? The anticipation of a reward from senior officers is part of the answer. Does this practice ensure confidence in the police service?

Whilst the service rewards such practice, habits begin to form and distortion begins to be created, we understand the activities that signal a good response in our minds and of the minds of others, so we cheat, we fabricate our activities. We wear the good clothes, we choose good friends, we choose the good car, we go to church and we get a good job. It all looks perfect. We create a haughty, arrogant attitude of perfection. People make assumptions about police officers, doctors, nurses and teachers. Good people, fine people and ethical. This is an assumption. **The only defining measure of our goodness is our altruistic intention. It is our altruistic intention (in the absence of reward and fear of punishment) and what we do on a day-to-day basis that makes ethical policing a reality.** Police officers who act with this distortion are merely going through the motions. The evidence of this distortion can be seen within the police service. How many times have you seen publicised initiatives that actually no one knows why they exist? So let's change our motivation to a more humane, heartfelt and in-touch intention.

The misunderstanding

I was talking to a cocky young man whilst walking on the beat one day. He approached me with a smirk on his face and said to me "I know something that you don't." With an arrogant look, he produced a wrap of white powder from his trouser pocket. "This is a legal high and there is nothing you can do to stop me from taking it." The young man laughed in my face and tried to taunt me with his remarks. It's legal you can't arrest me! The young man was full of contempt. I said to him, "Do you think that the law is designed to tell you what you can and can't do?" The male replied, "Yeah, that's right, and you can't do anything, I win and you lose." Calmly I said to him, "You are the law, you make your own decisions and live by them also. You can take your legal high and tell me if you felt good in the morning, try and convince me that it was a great idea." Weeks later, I attended a report of a teenage suicide; he unfortunately had played the ultimate price.

The legal understanding of law has been mixed up as a separate subject, written by clever lawyers and authorities. Many laws such as the human rights act have been misunderstood. Society has made an assumption that laws are there to protect them, and not a moral code to aspire to. Human Rights are also human aspirations, guidance that we should all aspire to and from the intention to practise day by day, year by year.

The street perspective

In terms of ethics in the 'here and now', a time and a place when a serving police officer has to make sense of an impending hostile encounter, there are two considerations that are worthy of noting and remembering.

Let's suppose that you have been sent out to work on a busy city centre. It's Saturday night and the guys and girls are dressed to impress, drunk, loud, cheeky, agitated and ready for some serious fun. You're standing next to a busy pub, the noise is deafening, there are people falling about, shouting, doing silly impressions, attempting to try your helmet on, asking for a photograph. The atmosphere is jovial but there is a sense of agitation in the air. It's 2am, you're alert and watching, being polite but watching, you know in your hearts of hearts that anything can happen. You notice a group of males walk into the public house. You notice their body language, chests puffed out, eyes fixed, looking back and forth, defensive and alert. The leader of the pack frequently touches his nose, sniffing, his communication is short and abrupt. He talks with hand signals, like an army corporal giving orders to his troops. The noise inside the pub is roof-shaking, the lights are whizzing, the room is ram packed, it's hot and slippery, and it's difficult to get to the bar. Outside the pub, a group of individuals are just hanging around, waiting to see if anything will happen. You know the type, avid boxing fans!

From the perspective of the biological stress response, this public house environment is stressful. The noise, lights, temperature, smell, cramped conditions, lack of space and feeling is creating the conditions for a stressful encounter.

The male who entered the public house had taken a wrap of amphetamines and has drunk a large amount of alcohol, he also hadn't eaten any food in the last six hours. His internal world is biologically stressed, agitated and aggressive.

You're the officer standing on your own, your colleague is chatting to a group of partygoers. You're feeling tired, a little hungry and cold. If you are really honest with yourself, you're also a little frightened. All of a sudden the side door opens and two males are ejected out of the pub. They begin to swing punches at one another, you hear the screams of a high-pitched voice. You look behind you and your colleague has her back to you. You know that you have do something, you know that you have to act. Your heart races and your adrenaline pumps. You grab hold of the most aggressive male and a struggle begins. You react, but you are overpowered and those aggressive males start to strangle and assault you. You are beaten across the face. Anger and resentment rush into your veins, "No way. I am not getting assaulted here." You react and kick out. Immediately and defensively you start throwing punches, for a moment it's a complete blur and you are starting to win the fight. Blood starts to seep across the floor. Flashes of fluorescent arrive and your colleagues manage to control the violence and hostility. You have the aggressive male pinned on the floor, you can't hear or speak and you're absolutely exhausted. Handcuffed, the male is shouting and swearing. You pick him up and take hold of his arm. Your colleague turns and faces you and says, "Are you OK? You're bleeding." You look in the mirror of the police van and see blood smeared across your face, bruising is beginning to surface below your eye. You look and feel a mess. Anger and rage simmer inside you. You leave the van and walk to the rear and the arrested male, spits at you and says, "You're fucking dead, next time." Boiling point is reached and a forceful impulse pulses near to your temples, you punch him twice in the face. You see red and his face squirms in pain.

Justification was allowed in the officer's mind 'Punishment must be administered when someone does something bad against you'. This is the officer's mental conditioning.

This time, there are dozens of witnesses and CCTV has captured the entire incident. You are compromised; you have assaulted a detained male in handcuffs.

Whilst you're sitting in handcuffs and waiting to be interviewed, the investigating officer says, "You have failed the disciplinary code and fallen below the required standard." You hang your head in shame. You play the entire incident around and around. You ask the question 'Why?' You have fallen below the standards and therefore are responsible for your actions.

How did this incident happen?
The events relating to this incident create anxiety and defensiveness. There is a relationship with regard to the location, offender, you and your inner feelings. The first point to make is that you are not separate from those events, you are indeed part of them and are actually merged with them.

Environment
The noise of the public house impaired your hearing; the lights caused disorientation and the people outside interfered with your communication. Your awareness at that time was hampered by the stressful environment.

Offender
The offender was intoxicated and biologically stressed and showed signs of arousal. His inner world was mixed with emotion.

You
You moved from a relaxed state of mind to a hypervigilant one. The behaviour of some of the individuals created tension; you were feeling a little anxious and a little frightened. Your past conditioning always supported the use of violence when confronted with violence.

The first point to make is that all of you share some similarities; you are all immersed in an unnatural circumstance where emotions and feelings are impaired and heightened. You were all party to external stressors (loud noise, bright lights, excessive heat, low blood sugar levels, extremes of temperature) internal stressors (fear, anxiety and worry). Looking at the incident from this perspective we can see that there is a bigger consideration to make. The only difference between you and the offender is the fact that you are sober and are wearing a uniform. You may have had all the police training and understand your legal duties inside out, but from a biological and emotional level, you're indeed very similar. This merging at a deeper level is called 'interdependence'. The merging of a variety of factors or conditions has culminated in an effect.

The environment, the offender, your support and your inner world brought you to a point of contact. The noise, tension, feeling, light and biological considerations placed you in a position of stress. A position of unfavourable disadvantage. Research shows that when a police officer is placed under considerable stress, the perception or use of force becomes reduced. A police officer's perception of judgement becomes considerably reduced. This reduction in perception created the conditions for a blind reaction by the officer. No thought was registered and neither was the feeling of anger and this culminated in ethical action: the action of assaulting a handcuffed detainee. The officer has fallen below the ethical standards. The wisdom is simple. We are as interdependent as the people that we are observing. To observe, we must pay attention to the policing environment, the offender, the potential victims and more importantly the effect that these factors have on our inner world. If we do this we are looking at our experience with the full faculty of experience. Just as a wave rises from the depths of the ocean, it needs conditions to help it form. It needs water, wind, direction and shallow water. Within its rising and forming, it naturally peaks, breaks and crashes onto the shore.

In the same way, the officer who became involved in this incident became involved in the emotion of anger. The anger isn't a separate dimension, when there is anger, the officer became the anger. In effect, he entered the angry world of the original angry male. But where there is rising there is falling, where there is formation there is destruction. Anger whilst being observed always changes and loses its energy, it never lasts and never strengthens. Every emotion, event, incident and experience is 'impermanent'.

The crashing of the wave of anger is, in effect, 'impermanence'. The natural law that we observe is simple 'events build through interdependence and events break up though impermanence'. How could the realisation of this natural law help the law-breaking officer?

The officer, with practice, may be able to observe such 'interdependence' whilst observing, we become aware of how anger and tension can affect our actions and behaviour. However, knowing that anger and tension has arisen within us, we become aware and observe the feeling of 'impermanence'. Having observed this inner feeling, we develop a form of unique observation. Within this space of unique observation, we have the freedom to choose our response. Anger and tension are bypassed but accepted for what they are.

The conditioning of reward or punishment becomes bypassed.

Think about the longstanding serving police officers that you work with. Do they react or are they calm in the face of confrontation?

Whenever you are faced with conflict either internally (in your own heart) or externally (out on the policing beat) always remind yourself that the conflict will eventually pass, it will not last. This is the natural law. Patience will always see past this experience. What happened to the officer? He was sacked.

Moral discipline and its perfect intention has a distinct relationship with negative and positive emotions. It is this factor of intention and emotion that really governs our actions of morality. There is a problematic reasoning with regard to right or wrong, because right and wrong always has a pairing with positive or negative emotions. It is far deeper than an intellectual understanding of what is right and wrong. A murderer knows that it is wrong to kill a human being, but the coupling of knowing of what is right and wrong is not enough to stop the murderous act. The murderer's mind has mixed itself with the state of mind that induces severe anger, resentment, hatred, rage and annihilation. It is the tide of negative emotion and total loss of control that results in the murderous act. In your police career, you would have interviewed many perpetrators. Whilst in interview think back to the time when they talked about their crimes, think about the body language that they presented. The explanation that people use exhibits the emotional component, "I hit her, because I am suffering from **depression**", "I threatened him, because **I was mad** at the situation", "**I feel** that they need to pay for what they have done". These daily admissions are emotional in nature and it is the disregard for the emotional nature of our being that causes us to break our imposed laws. At no time in my police career has any teacher of the law explained the relationship between the definition of law, its philosophies and our inner feelings.

Telling a lie

Think back to the time during your childhood when you told a blatant lie. The type of lie that covered your tracks, that made you look superior and ended up causing a whole lot of further trouble. Telling a blatant lie involves a sense of concealment, an act of internal tension.

Did you feel a sense of tension with your body? Did you gulp and swallow your lie in one full movement? Did you have butterflies in your stomach? Did you start to tremble and shake? Did you plan to cover your tracks? Were you anxious? Did the lie allow you to feel calm and peaceful? At that time when you told that lie, you knew intellectually that it is wrong to tell lies, but emotionally that early warning system of conscious feeling has overtaken intellectual reasoning.

Ethics is not an intellectual concept, where people in secure surroundings debate what is right and wrong. Ethics is a practice, it is not words, appearance or an initiative. It doesn't have a symbol, movement or framework, rather it is a deep-rooted intention, an understanding of emotion and the action of intuition that benefits ourselves and others. How many times have you heard those words 'think before you act'. Thinking is simply not enough, 'think and feel your emotions, then act'.

I have observed so much positive ethical conduct in the police officers of Bridgend. The officer who shows calmness, when confronted by an angry mob of drunken louts, who doesn't react to taunts and personal criticisms, who handles large amounts of seized property and money, returning it back to the public and benefitting the wider community. The officer who protects people from violent offenders, domestic violence victims and serial sex offenders. The officer who removes problem people from communities and changes people's lives. Ethical policing is all around, it is clear to see.

The following examples I have used are based in the sensory realm of experience, and they are similar to ordinary experience; however, the indulgence in such activity may give brief and fleeting pleasure, but that is it, and whoosh the experience is gone. **All these experiences are said to be 'impermanent'.** The harm that these temptations register, can last a lifetime of pain and suffering for not just you but your family and friends. When we make the realisation that temptation is brief and enjoyable in the short term, but is impermanent and induces long-term suffering, we realise that emotional temptation coupled with our need for wanting has the potential to cause our misfortune. We are said to be engaging in mindfulness and coupled with the awareness of moral discipline will, I can assure you, keep you happy, stress free and ensure you spend every penny of your hard-earned police pension.

The daily restraint of such emotional temptation is not a set of commandments. Such advice is not a 'should do or a must do' it is not a forced or a frustrated effort, it begins with the gentle understanding that such temptation has the ability to harm. If you are not entirely convinced with this ideology, write down your moral dilemma.

The first exercise within this chapter asked you to consider the activities that we avoid or secretly crave; we can begin to understand the emotional temptations that have more attraction or repulsion.

How does this exercise help the serving police officer?

This exercise will help to highlight, your subconscious decision-making process. You may be someone who craves success or status, you may be craving sexual relationships, you may be craving power and respect. Your motivation may be to avoid criticism or to avoid helping someone because they are 'bad'. This awareness will give you the insight to consider which types of internal struggles may develop into unwholesome behaviour. With this understanding, you then begin to understand the circumstances that may give rise to compromising your professional judgement and your integrity. I am not saying that you are going to compromise your professional integrity, but isn't being prepared for an internal battle justified? Circumstances change and policing is difficult. You wear your stab vest on a daily basis to protect yourself, in the same way, learning about your emotional drives may protect you from making harmful decisions.

Exercise 2

Write about the attached feeling of craving and its relationship on your inner feelings, state of mind and being. Recognise the time when such temptation changes and fades away, reflect on the quality of impermanence and how every temptation loses it power and foothold on your inner thoughts and feelings.

Experience	Reward or Punishment Is the reward of this activity driving your decision-making process?	Thoughts How long did the thinking process last for?	Feelings How did your feelings change?	Impermanence Did your experience change?
An attractive and seductive female drug dealer gives you her phone number				
You're alone with a detainee, he has been abusing you all day and now you have an opportunity to get your own back				
Consider your own experiences				
Consider your own experiences				
Consider your own experiences				

This exercise allows you to develop your inner experience.

Become the observer and hold the steadfast determination to observe such temptation. Try not to battle against powerful senses and watch them as if they were waves crashing into the shore. Notice by observing we are not reacting, we have control. With this inner awareness we begin to develop a more detached view of our policing experience.

The internal struggles

Police work by its very nature, exposes police officers to a variety of emotional temptations and opportunities for sensory happiness, more so than the average member of the public. It's difficult in that police officers are given a huge amount of public responsibility; however, they have to contend with powerful emotional temptations. It is difficult at times and moral struggles are faced daily, but let's make the opposing positive affirmations. These affirmations are not based on fear or punishment.

Sex

Go to any British town centre on a Saturday night and you will see gangs of women swooning around police cars. Most of the time the women are wearing very revealing clothing and are placing telephone numbers in officers' hands. The women are usually drunk and are enjoying themselves, and it is they who are chatting up the officers. Officers place themselves in difficult situations, false allegations are made against them, marital breakdown and relationship problems can develop from these sets of circumstances.

Do you secretly crave new and better relationships? Is this an area that could be your downfall? Is this reward going to benefit you in the long term?

The opposing altruistic intention: I am aware of the suffering caused by sexual misconduct. I am committed to cultivate responsibility and learn ways to protect the safety and integrity of individuals, couples, families and society. I am determined not to engage in sexual relations without love and a long-term commitment. To preserve the happiness of myself and others, I am determined to respect my commitments and the commitments of others. I will do everything in my power to protect children from sexual abuse and to prevent couples and families from being broken by sexual misconduct.

Harming others

The person who has been arrested threatened to "burn your house down and eat your children". After a violent encounter, the defendant has since calmed down. It is difficult to show restraint and even forgiveness to such a vile and sadistic person. Opportunities for retaliation are used. You could keep those handcuffs on for longer and tighten them, overzealous force could be used or you could isolate the person from food, water, care and vital medication.

Do you secretly crave power and control? Do you feel that punishing someone is justified? Is this an area that could be your downfall?

The opposing altruistic intention: I am aware of the suffering caused by physically harming others. I am committed to cultivating compassion and learning ways to avoid conflict. I am determined to only use force that is necessary.

Theft

Police officers are privy to being exposed to sums of money. A clear example of such activity is that of attending sudden deaths. Many old people don't have bank accounts and stuff money behind their beds. It would be very easy to place a couple of thousand pounds in your pocket. Drug enforcement is another area, where large amounts of cash can go missing. Information theft is another area where officers act as criminal informants, purposefully putting officers at risk and sabotaging police operations. Falsifying expenses claims, the finance clerk has no way of checking if you worked past five am.

Do you secretly crave a new life and all its comforts? Is this an area that could be your downfall? Is this reward going to benefit you in the long term?

Dishonesty

Dishonesty interlinks with many of the other temptations, even though it is not a temptation, it is usually part of the temptations intention. For example, having a relationship with a prostitute, will necessitate being dishonest to your family and co-workers.

Would you do anything to avoid criticism or to avoid helping someone because they are 'bad'? Would you act in a way that traps the 'bad'? Is this an area that could be your downfall? Is this reward going to benefit you in the long term?

The opposing altruistic intention: I am aware of the suffering caused by exploitation, social injustice, stealing and oppression. I am committed to cultivate loving kindness and learn ways to work for the well-being of people. I am committed to practice generosity by sharing my time, energy and material resources with those who are in real need. I am determined not to steal and not to possess anything that should belong to others. I will respect the property of others, but I will prevent others from profiting from human suffering.

Malicious speech

The power and influence that a police officer holds can give officers disproportionate amounts of power to controlling officers. If an officer holds a grudge against someone, they can torment many aspects of a person's life. For example, organising house raids, making up intelligence and acting on it, illegal stop and search, made-up statement facts and falsifying evidence. Blackmail and extortion are other examples.

Do you feel that you have the right to impose the law on others? Are you sometimes over controlling? Is this an area that could be your downfall? Do you feel that punishing someone is justified?

The opposing altruistic intention: I am aware of the suffering caused by unmindful speech and the inability to listen to others, I am committed to cultivate peaceful speech and deep listening in order to bring joy and happiness to others and relieve others of their suffering. Knowing that words can create happiness or suffering, I am committed to learn to speak truthfully, with words that inspire self-confidence, joy and hope. I am determined not to spread news that I do not know to be certain and not to criticise or condemn things of which I am not sure. I will refrain from uttering words that can cause division or discord, or that can cause the family or the community to break. I will make all efforts to reconcile and resolve all conflicts, however small.

Covetousness

Seeking worldly pleasures for the sake of them by the use of social standing. Taking free tickets, getting the children in the best local school, fixing contracts at the highest level, promotion for social standing and not for the benefit of the community. Seeking the very best equipment for your department and not considering the welfare of others. **Is this reward going to benefit you in the long term?**

Exercise 3

With courage and honesty, compile the following list. The example shows the possible link between thinking, feelings, policing circumstances and compromising behaviour. I am not stating that they all link together and follow through to unethical behaviour, it is the awareness of our thinking patterns that this exercise can develop.

Subconscious Thinking	Feelings	Policing Circumstances	Leading to Actions and Possible Behaviour	Outcomes and Consequences
"I really need some extra money, I can then order my new house extension and go on a well-deserved holiday" "I want, I want" "I need, I need"	"I will feel more complete, more contented and happy. This problem will go away, the kids will be happier and we can all enjoy a holiday" Feeling "happy, rewarded, accomplished, good and content" "no problems, everyone benefits"	After raiding a drug dealer's house, a relationship develops, you know one another as you used to played rugby together. Your old friendship begins to reform. You talk about the good old days and you are invited for a drink at the rugby club. After feeling a bit tipsy and seeing all the money that the dealer has, you enquire about what it is like living on the 'other side'. Your friend brags about the money and choices he has. You tell him that you have debts and financial problems	You are now beginning to become compromised. You have shown the dealer your vulnerabilities and he realises that he can solve your problem. He now becomes a 'good' person, someone who can solve your problem. He asks you for some information, in return you become financially rewarded. This process develops, you begin to take more risks and offer more information. The demands become larger and you're now putting people in danger	You tell the dealer that you can't go on anymore; a couple of heavies come around your house and threaten you and your family. They begin to blackmail you You become paranoid about going to work, you are waiting for someone to say something Stuck in a difficult position, you can't tell anyone. You begin to drink more and behave irrationally. Complaints begin to surface, the stress and pressure begins to rise

Subconscious Thinking	Feelings	Policing Circumstances	Leading to Actions and Possible Behaviour	Outcomes and Consequences
			You are now up to your neck in an unsolvable situation	You lose your temper at work and assault someone, you are investigated and you disclose to a close friend that you have been involved with a criminal gang. You seek help and just as you're getting better, you receive a visit from complaints and discipline. You're investigated and it is proven that you are corrupt

You lose your job

Depression sets in

Family breakdown |

Applying our altruistic intention

Interestingly, the UK Government made significant ethical changes to police officer powers. The arrest necessities of SOCAP 2005 now, for the first time ever, make the questioning of ethical practice a reality. When a police officer suspects an offence is being committed, the decision to arrest the suspect has to be justified by contemplating the necessity test. The test has the following criteria:

(5) The reasons are:

(a)   to enable the name of the person in question to be ascertained (in the case where the constable does not know, and cannot readily ascertain, the person's name, or has reasonable grounds for doubting whether a name given by the person as his name is his real name);

(b)   correspondingly as regards the person's address;

(c)   to prevent the person in question:
  (i)   causing physical injury to himself or any other person;
  (ii)   suffering physical injury;
  (iii) causing loss of or damage to property;
  (iv)   committing an offence against public decency (subject to subsection (6)); or
  (v)   causing an unlawful obstruction of the highway;

(d)   to protect a child or other vulnerable person from the person in question;

(e)   to allow the prompt and effective investigation of the offence or of the conduct of the person in question;

(f)   to prevent any prosecution for the offence from being hindered by the disappearance of the person in question.

(6)   Subsection (5)(c)(iv) applies only where members of the public going about their normal business cannot reasonably be expected to avoid the person in question.'

Our decision to arrest someone must be based on the evidence that we have collected and the contemplation of our ethical intention, the consideration of our intention allows us to make the correct decision.

The only defining measure of our goodness is our altruistic intention. It is our altruistic intention (in the absence of reward and fear of punishment) and what we do on a day-to-day basis that makes ethical policing a reality.

With that reiterated, notice that the arrest conditions actually bridge together with the above opposing affirmations (harming others, dishonesty), in particular the affirmation of not harming others. In our policing role, we are cultivating the intention to help others and then actually applying our intentions with our legal powers. This shift of consideration should prompt us to question our decisions and make a decision that benefits others, it also has the added protection of being able to stop unlawful arrests and put an end to corrupt and controlling police officers.

I have stated in previous chapters that police officers are exposed to physiological and psychological stressors. Research has documented that police officers show high levels of anxiety and depression. These components give rise to the opportunity for negative emotions to surface. The inner enemy of anger and resentment can take its foothold. If police officers are aware of what is right and wrong, why does each police agency have a designated department that monitors unethical behaviour? In this ethically fragile police career, how do police officers maintain ethical motivation? The answer lies in giving police officers time to relax, maintaining calmness and inner space. Positive morale is really the key to improving ethical motivation, positive emotions coupled with a pure ethical intention will allow the conditions of ethics to manifest. A great scholar and philosopher, Shantideva, said, "All the suffering in the world comes from seeking pleasure for oneself. All the happiness in the world comes from seeking pleasure for others." This timeless quote epitomises the group effort of improving morale. If the police service focuses on its staff, in a serious capacity, it will clearly benefit itself, happiness, success and simplicity will follow.

It is not an easy task to look at yourself in a revealing mirror, to watch your mind and notice its defilements. It takes constant effort, practice, patience and concentration to become mindful and create a wholesome intention that translates into positive ethical actions of body, speech and mind. When you begin to improve, reward yourself with gentle praise, you will notice a change in your view, composure, happiness and contentment, perhaps never experienced before.

With the consideration placed on ethical practice firmly set, the police service must make considerable effort to understand the activities that give rise to a rewards culture that may actually undermine ethical policing activities. Performance appraisals and the overt charting of performance statistics may have the opposing effect and actually pressurise police officers into acting with mindlessness, haste and selfish intention. It is these factors that widen the gap between the police and the communities in which we serve.

How do police officers introduce the daily practice of ethical motivation?

"The secret of health for both mind and body is not to mourn for the past, worry about the future, or anticipate troubles, but to live in the present moment wisely and earnestly."

Subconscious thinking	Feelings	Mindfulness	Leading to actions and possible behaviour	Outcomes and consequences
"I really need some extra money, I can then order my new house extension and go on a well-deserved holiday"	"I will feel more complete, more contented and happy. This problem will go away, the kids will be happier and we can all enjoy a holiday"	I am recognising my 'thinking mind'	I recognise that 'THINKING and FEELING' will eventually wither away, these experiences are impermanent and have no real grip over my decisions	I have returned to balance. I don't really need that extra money

Subconscious thinking	Feelings	Mindfulness	Leading to actions and possible behaviour	Outcomes and consequences
"I want, I want"	Feeling	I am transforming those inner ideas and words from "I want, I want", "I need, I need" to "THINKING"	I recognise that 'THINKING and FEELING' will eventually wither away, these experiences are impermanent and have no real grip over my decisions	I am not compromising my decisions or putting pressure on myself
"I need, I need"	"Happy, rewarded, accomplished, good and content"	I am recognising my 'bodily feelings'.		My policing world and its temptations have not been engaged, the line hasn't been crossed
	"No problems, everyone benefits"	I am transforming those inner ideas and words from "happy, rewarded, accomplished, good and content", "no problems, everyone benefits" to simply "FEELINGS"		

What form does continual awareness take? Firstly, it is awareness of all the tasks we normally complete in a day, especially the normal ones, the habitual ones. The ones we would normally do on automatic pilot. These range from brushing our teeth, drinking a cup of tea and routine tasks at work. Anything manual and physical needs to be done with awareness; done deliberately, purposefully, intentionally. Even closing drawers, opening cupboards should be done as if for the first time. A good technique to bring mindfulness to bear in our mundane tasks is to do them just a little more slowly and with careful deliberation. Another is to repeat the action that was done mindlessly. This sort of practice brings calmness and equanimity into our lives.

Sitting meditation

Begin sitting in a quiet place for a period of five minutes. Choose a comfy upright sitting posture. You could kneel, sit or even use a chair. Close your eyes and keep your back straight and comfortable. Focus on your breath and notice the rising and falling of your abdomen.

Body sensations (pain dull or sharp, itchy, prickly, heat, tightness, tenseness, goose pimples) when we experience such sensation, within your inner voice, label it 'SENSATIONS, SENSATIONS'.

Feelings (sadness, anger, resentment, jealousy, envy, pride, hatred, indifference, excitement, joy, calmness) when we experience such emotion, within your inner voice, label it 'FEELINGS, FEELINGS'.

Thoughts (planning, past, worrying, ruminating, self-doubt, self-pity, recurrent themes, a feeling of being stuck) when we experience such thoughts, within your inner voice, label it 'THINKING, THINKING'.

When a feeling, sensation or thought arises, attend to it with curiosity. Literally watch and observe. If you feel that your mind starts to wander, gently bring your attention to the feeling of breathing. Your breath is your anchor.

Policing 'The best practice'

Whenever we encounter conflict in our policing lives, pause, stop what you are doing and be still. If you are at a turning stone and you have to make a decision in a stressful situation, reacting will not help you. For example, if the aggressor has spat at you and offers an opportunity to fight, recognise your feelings first. Are you feeling angry, is there a gut-wrenching feeling in your belly? At that precise moment in time and space, pause and acknowledge. Within your inner voice say "FEELING ANGRY". Plunge your awareness into this feeling, breathe deeply and purposefully. As you take each breath, acknowledge this inner experience. Once again acknowledge the inner feeling and use your inner voice. With a deep, deliberate breath, label the feeling once again "FEELING ANGRY". Focus once again and become intimate with the feeling of anger, don't push it away or try and distract it. Stand in its grip and feel its might. Observe it, accept it and respect it. Our inner feeling of anger, wants to sweep you away like the outgoing tide, if you immerse yourself and become angry, it will sweep you away and control you. Observe anger for what it is, simply a rush of vibrational energy. In the heat of conflict, have you noticed that anger naturally eddies out and returns to calm? When you observed the inner voice and labelled your inner feelings for the third time, did you notice that the feeling, intensity and frequency of the emotion began to weaken slightly? Our emotions always weaken and slowly transform back to equilibrium and it is this realisation that can help you become alive to the present moment.

During our day-to-day working role, depending on the circumstances we may have a mixture of experiences including:

❑ Body sensations (pain dull or sharp, itchy, prickly, heat, tightness, tenseness, goose pimples) when we experience such sensation, within your inner voice, label it "SENSATIONS, SENSATIONS".

- ❑ Feelings (sadness, anger, resentment, jealousy, envy, pride, hatred, indifference, excitement, joy, calmness) when we experience such emotion, within your inner voice, label it "FEELINGS, FEELINGS".

- ❑ Thoughts (planning, past, worrying, ruminating, self-doubt, self-pity, recurrent themes, a feeling of being stuck) when we experience such thoughts, within your inner voice, label it "THINKING, THINKING".

Why do this practice?

Suppose the day is very busy and full of interruptions. If we now view these interruptions not as disturbances and nuisances, but simply accept them as the next thing to be done, we shall free ourselves of a lot of anger, frustration and stress. Suppose I am doing some written work, filling out forms or something, and someone approaches me for information. When they 'interrupt' me, with 'Excuse me', all I need say is, 'I'll be with you in a moment'. In that moment, I recollect where I am with the work I'm doing. To be aware is to remember. Then I turn to the questioner and devote myself to that request. Once the request is answered, I note that I have completed that task and go back to the written work where I have left a marker. No disturbance. No anger. No stress. Just moving from one job to another, creating a small space to recollect. If the person approaching is full of stress and bother, I don't become involved in that. I keep my attention to the problem and reassure the person.

Notice how by neutrally labelling our inner sensations, we are not jumping to conclusions, we are not judging, reacting, shouting or behaving. We are not projecting, minimising or blaming. We are simply watching and observing our minds, and the process of watching helps us develop inner space and it is the inner space that allows us to choose our response. Our minds have the ability to respond, now that's responsibility.

The mindfulness that I am describing can be developed through the practice of mindfulness meditation. Every day that you patrol the streets of your town, give rise to opportunity. The opportunity to become immersed in the present, to see the mirror of your own thoughts and feelings, and to simply acknowledge them and not to be swayed by such distractions. Police work in this sense becomes a gift. It is difficult being placed in demanding and stressful situations, but the benefits are far reaching, bringing patience, kindness, integrity and deep respect. You could go on in your career, being tossed around in the waves of negative emotion or you could choose to observe them for what they really are. It is this approach that I thank for policing and each problem that I see and its relationship that I have, now becomes an opportunity, a challenge to master our own minds.

Mindfulness has the added bonus of helping you feel less stressed, helping you make decisions clearer and assisting you to recognise powerful emotional temptations that may compromise your professional judgement. Mindfulness is the door to ethical decision making.

What does mindfulness achieve?

Honesty and integrity

Police officers are honest, act with integrity and do not compromise or abuse their position.

Authority, respect and courtesy

Police officers act with self-control and tolerance, treating members of the public and colleagues with respect and courtesy. Police officers do not abuse their powers or authority and respect the rights of all individuals.

Equality and diversity

Police officers act with fairness and impartiality. They do not discriminate unlawfully or unfairly.

Use of force

Police officers only use force to the extent that it is necessary, proportionate and reasonable in all the circumstances.

Duties and responsibilities

Police officers are diligent in the exercise of their duties and responsibilities.

Confidentiality

Police officers treat information with respect and access or disclose it only in the proper course of police duties.

Discreditable conduct

Police officers behave in a manner which does not discredit the police service or undermine public confidence, whether on or off duty. Police officers report any action taken against them for a criminal offence, conditions imposed by a court or the receipt of any penalty notice.

CHAPTER SUMMARY

- ❑ Identify with your thinking patterns. Do you use 'good' or 'bad' in appropriate situations.

- ❑ Does your using of 'good and bad' link with 'reward and punishment'?

- ❑ Identify what happens when you don't receive an appropriate reward or you're experiencing something that is 'bad'. How do you feel?

- ❑ Has your behaviour changed? Are you seeing 'bad' all the time?

8

REMEMBER THE POSITIVES

Urging employees to simply rethink their jobs was enough to drop absenteeism by 60 per cent and turnover by 75 per cent, a new University of Alberta study shows.

A 'Spirit at Work' intervention programme, designed to engage employees and give a sense of purpose, significantly boosted morale and job retention for a group of long-term health-care workers at the centre of the study.

"We discovered that people who are able to find meaning and purpose in their work, and can see how they make a difference through that work, are healthier, happier and more productive employees," said Val Kinjerski, a University of Alberta PhD graduate who co-authored the study and now works with organisations to cultivate productive workplaces.

The study focused on two groups of long-term health-care workers from two different care facilities in Canada. One group of 24 employees attended a Spirit at Work one-day workshop, followed by eight weekly booster sessions offered at shift changes. The workers were led through a variety of exercises designed to help staff create personal action plans to enhance spirit at work. They were asked to consider concepts like the deeper purpose of their work, being of service, appreciation of themselves and others, sense of community and self-care. The second group of 34 workers was offered no support programme.

The result for the intervention group was a 23 per cent increase in teamwork, a 10 per cent hike in job satisfaction and a 17 per cent jump in workplace morale. In addition, employer costs related to absenteeism were almost $12,000 less for the five months following the workshop than for the same period in the previous year. The employees also showed an increased interest in and focus on their patients.

The nature of police work is negative, the parade room is a place where negatives are expressed and aired. The conversation begins with, "If I was in charge I would do?" It's the people at the bottom who have that real everyday experience and can offer fresh insight. Every now again, when the going gets tough, it may be beneficial to reflect on your purpose and achievements. From a more personal perspective, I find it helps to reflect on the positives of policing.

Exciting role

There are many exciting jobs that are available within the police service. For the animal lover, there is a dog and horse section. The motoring enthusiast has much to choose from: off-road motorcycling, fast cars and motorbikes. Many people's hobbies can be incorporated into their day jobs: climbing, abseiling and underwater search. Some police officers love battle and confrontation and so firearms and riot police appeal. There is something for everyone. How many jobs can you have any number of careers within your service? If you plan your service and have a game plan you could in theory develop many different talents across the policing spectrum. A change is as good as a rest.

Freedom to roam

There aren't many jobs where you can roam around the towns and countryside, maybe visit a local beauty spot or even go for a walk. Some police officers cycle around the beat and enjoy the outdoors every day. Freedom is a great part of police work and it costs nothing. We are one of the only occupations that have the ability to be our own boss and still get a structured wage and career package. Sometimes, when I sit and watch the sunrise at a beautiful South Wales beach, it always dawns on me that I am very lucky to be witnessing Nature's beauty in total quietness. Night shifts are tough, but watching the sunrise is spectacular.

Insight knowledge

The beat officer has many opportunities to develop inner strength and has qualities that many aspire to have. The demands of our role can place us in many situations that give the opportunity for adoption of qualities such as courage, patience, humility, wisdom, kindness and compassion.

A long-term American study, tracked America's most successful men and women. The study concluded that the secret to success and happiness could be traced back to the way in which the subjects coped with setbacks. The development of coping strategies and the mental components of professionalism greatly improved the subjects' life experience.

Standing next to a cell door for a whole night shift and standing next to crazed detainee, hurling abuse and shouting at us, develops patience. Stopping a large-scale disturbance and risking your own life in a riotous, busy and dangerous town centre requires courage. Applying attention to detail and tracking down a violent criminal making sure no stone is unturned and the offender is convicted requires wisdom. Helping a known criminal, come to terms with being a victim of crime requires absolute and unconditional kindness. Helping a victim of domestic abuse when you know that she will be back with her partner, requires considerable compassion. There are many examples to choose from, and you could reflect on the qualities that you have developed over the last couple of years. Police officers, by definition, have real insight by the nature of what we see, hear and experience. We understand society and the complexities of what is really going on within our communities.

Making a difference

We do make a difference, no matter how difficult our jobs are, we meet people who have experienced terrible tragedy and we can help them in many practical ways. Most of the calls that we deal with are not so urgent and there is a sense that people are co-dependent and could actually help themselves. But now and again, we meet people who really need us to intervene and listen. It's those

times we really can make a positive difference. We tend to look at the people we deal with through our own values. The court system does this on a daily basis. It considers the crime in isolation to the bigger picture. A car thief who was recently convicted for stealing a car, was given 14 days' imprisonment. But what the court is not aware of is the bigger chaotic picture that this person is involved in. The thief is an abuser, he hammers his family and has done some dreadful things, he plays music all day and has caused considerable distress to his neighbours. He doesn't work, he sleeps with many women and he has lots of children scattered about the place, but hasn't fathered any of them. When the bigger picture is adopted it gives us a call to urgency, so we really do get the remand application correct, and we lock them up!

Sport and groups

Police officers are always doing something, raising money for charity, participating in sporting events. There are numerous sports and groups that can accommodate your interests. It's these events that foster team working and deeper friendship and camaraderie.

Friendship

I went to call with a colleague of mine, PC Gerry Mckay. The incident was a routine criminal damage call. Some local children had kicked the panels of an elderly person's outer fence. The elderly gent was upset; we later discovered that he had lost his wife some weeks ago. Gerry sat the man down, went into his kitchen and made him a cup of traditional tea from a traditional tea pot. As we sat, we chatted about the good old days and he told us some war stories. Gerry popped next door to speak to the neighbours, or so I thought. I could hear 'bang, bang, saw, saw'. I looked out of the window and saw him fixing the fence. Ten minutes later, Gerry came into the lounge and said, "There we are, good as new". The elderly gent was absolutely thrilled to bits. I thought to myself, "Now that's community policing. I can't believe what I had just seen". This is just one of the stories that shows what great people there are around us in the police service. It's people like Gerry who we can rely on, people who give no less than one hundred percent and are a friend for life.

Gratitude

Every once in a while, I think it is important to ponder on how fortunate we are. When I think about and listen to the stories about my colleagues I genuinely hold them in high esteem. Glance through your pocket book and consider the past six months. In a six-month period, a police officer can witness a variety of incidents. From town centre riots to chatting to market traders, the job is very varied. When the doom and gloom has set in and it becomes tense and volatile, who is on our shoulder protecting us? It's our friends and colleagues. They protect us, fight for us, stick up for us and help us. The danger that comes with the job seems less of a burden when it is shared. Our colleagues are very special, sometimes we forget their sacrifices and the courage that they show on a daily basis. People say, "This generation don't help people anymore". I don't share this view, the people I work with do more than just help, they do it with courage, determination and humility. Spend time thinking about your colleagues and the courage they have shown to keep you safe and well.

CONCLUSION

9

Police work is difficult and challenging, and will always be difficult and challenging. Our policing world requires extra physical and emotional investment to get the job done. Getting the job done comes at a cost, a human cost. We place ourselves in confrontational extremes and we call this 'going to work'. The gap that policing creates needs to be filled with stress-relieving practices and proactive morale boosting initiatives. If we are to be true to ourselves and our colleagues we would have come to the conclusion that this is not someone else's job, it begins with you. You and only you can ask the question: "What am I prepared to do to improve my own morale and reduce my colleagues stress levels?"

Your daily ethical contribution is your first consideration. Learning about your emotional drives will serve you well to identify times of ethical temptation. This has to be your first consideration, it will keep you in a job first and foremost. Next comes learning about your maladaptive coping strategies. Do you reach for food, cigarettes or alcohol? Within the scope of identifying your personal stressors you can begin to introduce some of the stressor-reducing practices that I have discussed in the first chapter. This small practice will serve to reduce your personal stressors and reduce the pull towards maladaptive practices.

The psychological and emotional pressures of police work can be attended to by the scientifically proven method of Mindfulness-based Stress Reduction. Once you have learnt this technique, it costs nothing to practice and develop. Workplace stress can be easily managed by attending to demand, communication, support, role, change and relationships. Every once in a while, reward yourself and spend some time thinking about the many positives that are as a result of doing a difficult job. Focus on the long term, take a slow step toward a calm, balanced and happy police career. Stay safe and enjoy your pension, you deserve it.

Putting the information I have presented into practice is no easy task. The last section aims to put the current research into practice by the means of a station self-assessment.

Stress Assessment

Has each member of staff had a presentation on the effects of stress?

Does each member of staff know how to assess personal stress?

Does the organisation have access to a reliable and tested online stress questionnaire? A questionnaire accessible from every workplace computer.

Has every member of staff been given a copy of Morale Matters?

Welfare

Does each member of staff know what welfare and counselling do?

Does each member of staff know what help is available?

Does each member of staff know their welfare, employment, maternity, sickness and diversity rights?

Is there a clear and up-to-date welfare notice board?

Do staff have a say in their annual leave allocation? Is there flexibility when requesting time off or swapping of shifts?

Environment

Does your police station have an area set aside for relaxation?

Does your police station have adequate food preparation areas?

Does your police station have an exercise area? Are you encouraged to use this facility? Does each member of staff have adequate locker space?

Is there adequate light in each room? Does your station have blue light as standard? Is each room clean and tidy? Are there plants within each room?

Have 'act now' posters been removed? Are there tea-making facilities? Is the police station comfortable?

Communication

Are regular face-to-face meetings held with all staff? Are you encouraged to report on a daily basis issues that you are experiencing?

Is there an open method of communication between management and staff?

Are staff and morale issues incorporated into daily briefings? Are staff dictated to during shift meetings? Is there a process that quashes daily rumours?

Personal Stress Management

Have you received training in stress reduction techniques?

Have you been issued with earplugs for noisy areas?

Do you carry all the necessary personal protective equipment?

Is your home modified for night shift sleep?

Do you have a stress-reducing routine?

Do you have a personal and adaptable exercise routine?

Do you plan your off-duty time? Do you have a family calendar? Do you have freeze-dried food in your locker? Do you have a spare uniform and spare set of clothes? Do you make time for positive thinking? Do you have a healthy work life balance?

At Work

Do you make time for face-to-face communication?

Do you make time to get to know staff members?

Do you sit and eat with your team members? Are your meal breaks factored into your working day?

Are team building activities actively encouraged?

Are staff praised and rewarded?

Do you make time for self-reflection?

Do you plan as well as you could do? Do you manage your time well?

Is unacceptable behaviour challenged? Is there a confidential reporting system? What is being done on a daily basis to improve officer morale?

Do police officers have access to time-out opportunities?

Demand

Are the current demands equally shared?

Are difficult and traumatic incidents planned for?

Do officers have a say in what work they do?

Can the officer request time away from work following a difficult incident?

SUMMARY

- individual emotional responses – police officers who relied on negative or avoidant coping mechanisms reported both higher levels of perceived work stress and adverse health outcomes;

- organisational culture – including exposure to critical incidents, workplace discrimination, lack of cooperation among co-workers, and job dissatisfaction correlated significantly with perceived work stress;

- workplace issues – such as the demands of work impinging upon home life, lack of consultation and communication, lack of control over workload, inadequate support and excess workload in general.

- Physiological stressors, such as hunger, thirst, sleep, rest, temperature and light, change your thinking and behaviour. However, you do have many opportunities to counteract their effect.

- Slow down and pace yourself.

- Observe your policing experiences using the full faculty of awareness.

- Take time to reflect and pause.

- Learn how to make use of mindfulness meditation.

- Identify times of emotional distress be gentle with yourself.

- Take advantage of all support that is available.

- Take an active role in your recovery, learn about ways in which you can support yourself.

- Identify with your thinking patterns. Do you use 'good' or 'bad' in appropriate situations.

- Does your using of 'good and bad' link with 'reward and punishment'?

- Identify what happens when you don't receive an appropriate reward or you're experiencing something that is 'bad'. How do you feel?

- Has your behaviour changed? Are you seeing 'bad' all the time?

Neville Evans is a serving frontline police officer in a British police force. He has over ten years of frontline policing experience and has won numerous awards for community policing. In conjunction with his policing career, he has managed a community-based fitness programme and has bettered the lives of hundreds of people, keeping them active and free from illness. He has a degree in health and exercise science and has mentored many people. Neville is the author of 'Safe – your complete guide to domestic abuse'. This publication has supported thousands of families across the UK and is an excellent guide to helping survivors of domestic abuse. He has also written a detailed self-help book for teenage victims of bullying.

Neville's website www.talkandsupport.co.uk has numerous supporting videos, and details of his books and products can be found there.

Reordering

Additional copies of Morale Matters are available from our website www.talkandsupport.co.uk. Please contact us by email and we can arrange quantity discounts by request. Our book can be purchased from Amazon.

Email: evansneville@aol.com